YOUR HOME OFFICE
IS PRESENTED IN ADDITIONAL ASSOCIATION WITH

Do you plan to run a business from home or use a room there for occasional freelance work? *Your Home Office* has been written for you, from the experience of working from home. It describes how to choose and set up an office that will enable you to work efficiently, productively and profitably.

If you already have a home office, the useful tips may help you to improve its organisation. A well-planned home office can reduce the time spent on admin for which you do not get paid. Modern technology can provide the tools to run a complete office in the home, leaving you free to get on with the real business.

The benefits of the most useful equipment for the small office are spelled out, together with price ranges and the ease or otherwise of installation and use. Do not be without this invaluable guide when you set up on your own.

Peter Chatterton is a successful consultant who helps businesses, from one-man bands to large corporations, to use office equipment profitably.

Peter Chatterton is an independent consultant whose views are represented in this book; he has no connection with the advertised products or services

THE EXPRESS
YOUR HOME OFFICE

The Express Guides

The Express and Kogan Page have joined forces to publish a series of practical guides offering no-nonsense advice on a wide range of financial, legal and business topics.

Whether you want to manage your money better, make more money, get a new business idea off the ground – and make sure it's legal – there's an Express Guide for you.

Titles published so far include:

Be Your Own Boss!
How to Set Up a Successful Small Business
David McMullan

How to Cut Your Tax Bill Without Breaking the Law
Grant Thornton, Chartered Accountants

Great Ideas for Making Money
Niki Chesworth

Network Marketing
David Barber

You and the Law
A Simple Guide to All Your Legal Problems
Susan Singleton

Your Money
How to Make the Most of it
Niki Chesworth

The Women's Guide to Finance
Tony Levene

How to Cope with Separation and Divorce
A Guide to Married and Unmarried Couples
David Green

Buying Your First Franchise
Greg Clarke

The Daily Express Investment Guide
Practical Advice for Making the Right Choice
Tony Levene

Buying a Property Abroad
Niki Chesworth

How to Sell More
A Guide for Small Business
Neil Johnson

Readymade Business Letters that get Results
Jim Douglas

Available from all good bookshops, or to obtain further information please contact the publishers at the address below:

Kogan Page Ltd
120 Pentonville Road
London N1 9JN
Tel: 0171 278 0433
Fax: 0171 837 6348

THE EXPRESS
YOUR HOME OFFICE

*A Practical Guide to Using
Technology Successfully*

REVISED SECOND EDITION

PETER CHATTERTON

**KOGAN
PAGE**

First published in 1995
Revised second edition 1997

Adapted from the author's book, *Technology Tools for Your Home Office.*

Kogan Page Limited
120 Pentonville Road
London N1 9JN

British Library Cataloguing in Publication Data

A CIP record for this book is available from the British Library.

ISBN 0-7494-2234-3

Typeset by Kogan Page
Printed and bound in England by Clays Ltd, St Ives plc

Contents

What is a Personal Number?

A Personal Number is one number for life, that allows you to receive calls wherever you are.

One number that puts all your calls through to you, whether at home, in the office, on the mobile, or away at any location. As long as there is a phone nearby, you'll never miss an important call.

One Number For Life

Your clients and friends will only need one number to contact you, even though you might move home, move office or change job.

A Personal Number is not connected to a particular phone or address, it is connected to a business or individual. No matter where you are, you'll always be in, without revealing your location.

Your number can never be stolen, you have your own security code, which prevents fraud and unauthorised use.

All Dovecoat Personal Numbers are prefixed with the prestigious 07000 dialling code, then the normal six digits – which can even be a number of your choice.

This advanced communication technology is ideal for both business and private users. Personal Numbering is predicted by Oftel, the industry watchdog, to be an area of rapid growth, with over 500,000 Personal Number holders by the year 2000.

How do 07000 Personal Numbers Work?

The beauty is that the latest computer technology makes Personal Numbers so easy to use.

You keep all your existing telephone lines and numbers. Your Personal Number will sit on top of any phone number of your choice. Using a simple code, followed by your pin number, calls are forwarded to whichever phone you choose. This can be done using any phone at any location. No installation of equipment is required.

The phone number you link to will still operate as usual on it's own normal number, but it wil also adopt your Personal Number for as long as you want it to. Callers hear no difference from traditional calls, just a normal ringing tone.

Reroute Your Calls to Any Phone

You can change the destination of your Personal Number as often as you wish. Instead of having to chase after your calls, you can relax in the knowledge that your calls will be chasing after you.

Calls can be forwarded to a mobile phone in exactly the same way as you would with an ordinary phone. You also have the flexibility to transfer to a landline to avoid mobile blackspots.

Should you wish not to be disturbed, you can divert your calls to an answer phone or a colleague. An optional messenger service and nationwide pager service are available for a small extra charge.

What Are the Benefits?

Dovecote Personal Numbers give you the confidence and freedom to travel without missing a vital call. We offer a flexible service to suit your changing needs, with full support and back-up.

• Four million numbers change, for one reason or another every single year. Your Personal Telephone Number will never change.
• Your friends and business contacts still certainly appreciate you having only one number
• If you move home or office there is no need to worry about changing your telephone number
• You can be contacted on your Personal Number, not only in the UK, but also abroad.

And in business . . .

Advertisements, business cards, stationery and vehicle liveries will never become outdated. If you are working at home, you can use your Personal Number to avoid giving callers your private line.

The Cost Advantages . . .

No surprise bills, just one annual payment. There is no charge to the Personal Number holder when diverting calls to a landline.

What will a Personal Number Cost?

After a one-off connection fee, all you pay is a small annual service charge.

Faxes For The

Canon has been at the forefront of many technological developments in the fax market and has developed a range of fax machines specifically for the home office.

For those who require a fully-automated home office, Canon offers two multifunctional machines, the MultiPASS 10 and MultiPASS C30. These are essentially four business machines rolled into a single, simple-to-use, desktop unit.

Plain-paper fax (either standalone or linked to a PC), plus copying, printing and scanning facilities are provided. Both machines are great space savers and cost less than half the price of buying these peripherals separately. And, the Multi-PASS C30 offers the added

benefit of colour printing too

Canon's specificall designed software, Mult PASS, allows the MultiPAS: 10 and MultiPASS C30 t be controlled from the PC when installed unde Windows/Windows 95 Faxed documents receive on the PC via MultiPASS, have the same quality as the original document when printed out. The data can be inserted into other PC files and edited. Paper and ink consumption is reduced, as a hard copy

The Canon

of the fax is not needed fc sending, and receive documents can be viewe directly on the PC's screen.

)ffice At Home

If a simple standalone x is all that's required, anon offers the B100 and 110 Bubble Jet faxes, hich print incoming fax essages directly onto andard cut sheet A4 aper. These can be used s working documents,

:S C30 Fax

won't curl or fade and can be filed away easily.

In addition, the B110 offers a built-in digital answerphone so that both faxes and phone calls are never missed. Messages are received automatically – faxes re printed onto paper and bice messages are corded in the fax memory for accessing or playing back through any tone dialling telephone.

Customer Care

Canon's home office fax range offers improved quality of faxed documents using Canon's renowned Bubble Jet print technology, reduced running costs, faster operator time and reduced call costs.

To get the most from your fax, it is worth investing the time to get to know these features. To make this easier, Canon offers its customers a free helpdesk service, providing advice on any kind of fax question. In addition, a 1 year on-site warranty is provided with all Canon's home office fax products.

For sales enquiries/ brochures: 0500 246246.

A Burst of Colour!

Canon's MultiPASS C30 provides a colour printer, fax, scanner and copier in a single desktop unit, for less than half the price of four separate peripherals. Control from the PC is enabled using Canon's unique MultiPASS software for Windows/Windows 95.

Quality is the key to presentation and the printer emulates the Canon BJC 4100, ensuring that documents look professional, eye-catching and provide the answer to high impact reports.

The MultiPASS C30 provides advanced fax features with a memory that can be upgraded, to ensure that as the user's requirements grow, so too does the fax machine.

Designed for today's environment the Multi-PASS C30 is an afford-able multi-functional machine with a built-in colour printer.

FOR FURTHER INFORMATION PLEASE CALL 0500 246 246
MultiPASS™ is a registered trademark of Canon inc.

The MultiPASS C30 Fax

1

Why you should read this book

Several years ago I decided that I wanted more freedom to work on my own, rather than for other people. I took the plunge, admittedly with some apprehension, and set up a home-based office. Since then there hasn't been a single regret, except that it should have been sooner!

At first, it seemed a relatively simple matter to set up an office by using one of the rooms in my house. Over a period of time, it became apparent that there were quite a number of practical things to think about. For instance, it can be easy to get cut off from the world without the everyday contact of office life, and family and friends can provide unwanted interruptions when you are trying to concentrate on your work. On a rather more mundane level, a friend provided a useful reminder that household insurance, in many cases, does not provide cover for business use of equipment such as computers.

Your Home Office has been written from the experience of working from a home office for over six years. It describes how to choose and set up an office that will enable you to work efficiently and productively and provides useful tips to avoid some of the pitfalls of home working.

Just because you work from home does not mean that you can avoid having to comply with rules and regulations, whether they are from the local planning office, your landlord or mortgage lender. Some of the more common rules and regulations that you might encounter are described, together with useful guidelines on dealing with insurance and tax issues.

It is only recently that setting up a home office has become a practical and economic proposition, whether you are self-employed or working for a company. A major reason for this is the availability of (relatively) low-cost office equipment – particularly technology tools – to help with all the office jobs that we normally take for granted – letters, reports, brochures, bookkeeping, presentations – and so on.

IF YOU WORK FROM HOME, WILL YOUR INSURANCE BE WORKING FOR YOU?

by Neil Andrews of ITT London & Edinburgh

So you've had the idea to make you a millionaire. You;ve invested in equipment and technology vital to your success. Staff have been recruited and you have converted your property to accommodate your business.

Well, now the hard work really starts. The initial effort will count for little until your business starts to succeed. With so much relying on you and your equipment, you will have given some though to insurance. However, as you are working from home you might assume the household policy you took out years ago, will cover your business as well.

The fact is, you are wrong to assume this! By running your business from home or by working at home at any time, you must re-consider your home insurance. If you do not contact your insurer to explain about the business use, it is likely that your policy will be worth little more than the re-cycled paper on which it has been printed.

Worse still, if you wait until you need to make claim before you mention it, you will almost certainly find that your claim is reduced or even refused. This could happen even if the claim you make does not raise directly from the business use of the property.

Unfortunately, you will probably find that when you pick up the phone to advise of this minor chAnge in your circumstances, your problems are not immediately solved. Most insurers offer little or no cover for homes used wholly or partly for business. The outcome is likely to be insufficient insurance or the cancellation of the policy.

Despite this, don't be tempted by the idea of ignoring the issue. With so much time, money and effort invested in your business, it would be unwise to take such a gamble. So what should you do?

Well, in the same way that you looked to a specialist for each of your business needs, the same is true of insurance. Standard household policies usually represent excellent value for normal homeowners. However, you now need to consider that your home, or part of it, is your workplace and you need to insure it as such. The fact is, your business is special and your insurance policy has to be specially tailored to take account of this.

Personal computers, modems, fax machines, photocopiers and mobile telephones are essential to today's business people. You will have considered protecting this equipment and home security may well be in your plans. However, most measures, including the non specialist insurance policies, look only at the short term losses you are likely to suffer.

If you have your equipment stolen by a hi-tech thief with hi-tech contacts, you would claim and your insurer would arrange to replace it. However, how would your business cope without the equipment if you had to wait several weeks for replacements? The interruption to your business could be very costly. Work could be disrupted. Orders may be missed and clients lost. If your PC is stolen and you haven't backed up a vital disk, all sorts of files essential to your work may never be found.

Working from home has a great many advantages. But have you ever stopped to consider how even the smallest events would affect you if your business is a home? If you worked in an office during some of the great storms of recent years and your journey to work was halted by fallen trees and power lines, most people were happy to take the day off! If you work from home and a storm brings down the phone and power lines, where would that leave your business?

What about visitors to your home? When these visitors are business acquaintances or customers, have you considered that you will also need public liability insurance? If you employ staff to work from your home, you will know that the law requires you to have employer's liability cover. If you make anything, you will need products liability. If you deliver stock to your customers, you may require goods in transit cover.

And what if you need to claim? A lengthy claims process with endless forms won't help you do your business. A claims service with 24 hour emergency assistance and a telephone claim registration line will. Approved tradespeople, guaranteed work and fast service will get you back in business before other insurers have even sent you a claim form.

Let's face it, you need to think about **FastTrack Home-Work**, the specialist insurance from **ITT London & Edinburgh**.

As FastTrack Home-Work is not constrained by the usual home insurance rules, we can underwrite you a policy as individual as your business. And **ITT London & Edinburgh** was one of the first insurers to offer this type of specialist policy, you can rely on our experience. And if you need to claim, we'll make it as painless as possible!

To find out more about **FastTrack Home-Work** with the **FastTrack Claims Service**, and to get a quotation, please contact:

VECTIS INSURANCE SERVICES LTD

Telephone: 01983 298311
Fax: 01983 296508

Alternatively, complete the enclosed **FREEPOST** card and return it to **Vectis Insurance Services Ltd**.

When you're working from home,
get *FastTrack Home-Work* to work for you!

Sure, this can all be done without technology. Stationery can be printed at the local print-shop. Secretarial, faxing and telephone answering services can all be bought-in. There is no shortage of accountants to do the bookkeeping, and public relations (PR) companies will gladly send out mail-shots to press and customers. But all this is expensive, and, it is time-consuming. The old saying goes that 'time is money' – if you spend all your time running the office, there is none left for doing work that will pay the bills. Technology can provide the tools to run a complete office in the home – a means to an end – allowing you to get on with your real business.

The same applies if you are working for a large company and are able to take advantage of flexible home-working opportunities. Bookkeeping and public relations might not be high on the list of requirements, however, communicating and sharing information with your company will most certainly be necessary to overcome the problems of isolation when working from home.

The personal computer (PC) provides most of the tools necessary for running your home office. Don't let the traditional image of computers put you off. They have changed rather like cameras have. Ten years ago, cameras were complex beasts, requiring the aperture, focus and the speed to be set, the light to be read and so on; now, the modern camera does all this for you, *and is cheaper than at any time.* Similarly, computers are now affordable and easier to use.

The personal computer is *just that* – it is a personal productivity tool and *it is in your control* – not a big corporation's. What's more, manufacturers have at last realised that the majority of users are not computer programmers; they need easy-to-use tools ('user-friendly' is their favourite expression). In fact, many people find PCs simpler to operate than video cassette recorders and, with certain exceptions, they come with clearer instruction books (how many times have you recorded the wrong programmes at the wrong times on your video cassette recorder?). Furthermore, the PC can be tailored to suit different business needs and can give freedom for an alternative and flexible lifestyle. Combined with the new products and services offered by the telephone companies, this flexibility can even extend to a fully 'portable' office – making business abroad a realistic proposition for the small business.

One of the factors that puts many people off using the PC is having to learn to type. This is not such a big deal. Computers offer many advantages over the typewriter – they are forgiving of mistakes and will even help you to learn speed typing, without necessarily taking a typing course. Through continual use, it is possible quickly to reach speeds that, even though they might not make you a touch-typist, can certainly be adequate for the rate at which you can compose the words. Having said that, it is worth learning the basics of typing – fingering position and so on – as it will stop you getting into bad habits which, as time goes on, are more and more difficult to shake off.

Visiting friends and acquaintances often comment 'I didn't realise you could do all that so cheaply', and, through that realisation, has been born the idea for many small businesses. One of my biggest 'success stories' was from a friend who had an idea for a business selling low-cost accessories to the motor-trade. His key technology requirement was for an accounting system that would allow him to send prompt invoices, keep customer records, chase money with regular statements, send flyers to existing customers on new products and prepare all the accounts ready for auditing. He reckons that his computer system has increased his profits by £25,000 in two years from clerical staff costs and accountancy fee savings, and the increased sales from being able to mail-shot his customers easily. Using his accounts software also taught him to fully understand and have confidence with bookkeeping and accounting practices.

On the other end of the scale, a journalist friend who worked for one of the 'heavy' newspapers wanted to do some freelance work. He bought a low-cost PC with word-processing software and a printer, which made it realistic for him to work in the evenings as well as holding down his day-time job. It did not save him the kind of money that my motor-trade friend saved, but it did enable him to get copy out in limited hours, which eventually led to a full-time freelance career. He reckons this would probably not have been possible if his only tool had been the typewriter.

Your Home Office has been inspired by such experiences. It has been written from the business perspective and focuses particularly on the benefits of common-sense uses of office equipment, in particular, modern technology. Most books on this subject make unfulfilled promises of 'simplifying the technology jargon'. This one is intended to answer the questions 'What is possible?' and 'How to set it up?' without the techno-speak. It will help you to decide what you really need as opposed to what the jargon-ridden salesman wants to sell you. It will point out the business reasons for investing in technology and show how your investment can pay back in increased profitability. It will show how you can keep your operating costs low (printing your own quality stationery and brochures, etc), how to increase your sales (hitting customers with regular mail-shots and press releases and so on) and how to bookkeep and exercise strict financial control (such as instant invoicing, timely and forceful reminder statements and cash flow projection). It also illustrates the benefits of using technology to communicate and share information with others, for example, other home-based businesses or larger companies.

A businessman once remarked that technology was all very well but it could not solve the problem of answering the phones with a friendly voice when you are out. Having a telephonist is the ideal, but can you afford the cost? In most cases the answer is probably no. There are now many low-cost alternatives such as answerphones and paging services which will alert you (wherever you are) when a message is left. You can even divert your office calls to a mobile phone. These technologies are now used in both small and large businesses and, as people get used to them, they are realising that there can be many advantages over leaving messages with people, which don't always get passed on quickly or accurately.

Your Home Office is not intended to make a computer genius out of you or tell you how to use specific products (there are plenty of other books that do that well). But it will provide practical tips and examples to give you confidence in getting to grips with the nuts and bolts. You can then make good decisions and plan your learning and use of equipment in a way that suits you. The book explains the basics of the technologies and, if you are already familiar with many of them, you may want to gloss over those sections. On the other hand, it is not a bad thing to read all of the book even if you think you are an expert.

Many people associate home working with the negative images that the media tend to portray, emphasising problems such as the lack of human contact found in a more conventional office environment. *Your Home Office* finishes with a chapter on practical tips for home working that will not only help you to avoid such problems, but will also help you to take advantage of the benefits of home working and create a new lifestyle that others will come to envy in time.

2

Setting up your home office

It's not unusual to hear people who work in traditional jobs say that 'they take their work home with them'. This is all very well and good (indeed, it may reflect flexible working arrangements), but it is not uncommon to find that these people have difficulty in separating work and home life. This can obviously be even more problematical for the home worker who will need to make a very clear distinction between the two.

Using a separate office from the rest of the home is one easy thing you can do to help this separation, provided you have the room. This not only helps psychologically, but it is also practical to keep all home and office equipment and materials totally separate. It can also prevent major domestic rows!

Choosing the office area

The ideal home office would probably be a detached large room with its own kitchen and wash room facilities. This would ensure that you don't disturb members of your household and, probably just as important, they don't disturb you. It would also mean that you would not need to enter the rest of your home for things like making coffee and this can help save you from domestic distractions. Unless you already have such a room waiting for you to move into, this is neither practical nor economic. Building one would be costly and time-consuming and require compliance with a string of planning regulations, and this is the last thing you need when your attention should be on developing your business!

If your office is going to be used solely by yourself, and you do not intend inviting business contacts such as customers and suppliers to visit you, the choice of office area is made simpler as you do not need to consider making a good impression on others. You should, however, choose a room taking into account a number of considerations:

Budget's homework revolution

London's premier supplier of office furniture, Budget Furniture PLC, has been established for over 20 years. During this period there have been a number of significant changes in the industry. Much more emphasis is now placed on the ergonomic design of workstations and office seating, for example, and employers have a statutory duty to provide their employees with safe and 'user friendly' equipment. Colour fashions are constantly changing, and the advent of electronic information technology has resulted in a radical redesign of workstations.

The latest trend is towards home working. It is not just the one person businesses with an office in the spare room who are setting the trend. Some of the largest corporations in the country are encouraging workers, particularly those involved in information technology, to work from home. Companies provide all of the necessary equipment for the home office and thus make big savings in their overhead costs.

A workstation for the home can be no more than a simple desk placed in a corner of the lounge; or it could be a suite of office furniture in a room entirely dedicated to office work. there are also suites of modular furniture available which can be integrated with bedroom furniture to give the room a planned and 'fitted' look.

Examples of many home office furniture ranges can be viewed at Budget's spacious showroom in Herne Hill, south-east London. Visitors are always welcome, and there is ample free parking. For the home shopper who is unable to get to the showroom Budget Furniture produces a variety of excellent product catalogues, including a special Home Office catalogue. You can make your choice of the home office furniture which best suits your needs and then order by 'phone, fax or mail. There is almost certain to be a workstation in a style, colour and price to suit each individual customer, as the Budget range is vast. And, of course, Budget's friendly and experienced sales staff will be pleased to give you as much help and advice as you need.

Furniture is supplied in knocked-down form ready for easy self-assembly, and delivery is free to the UK mainland (excluding the Scottish Highlands).

Noise

It's surprising how people can get used to typical external noises such as those from traffic. However, if you are going to spend a lot of time in your home office, it would be preferable to choose a room that has the minimum of noise intrusion from outside. Possibly of more importance is to avoid areas where you will hear your neighbours, and remember that school holiday time could mean that gardens will be buzzing with distracting noise from children. While double glazing can help to reduce the problem, it won't provide you with fresh and cool air in the hot summer months! Internal noise can be just as, or even more, distracting and your ideal room should be well away from any noise that is likely to arise when you work, such as from children's play rooms.

Heating and ventilation

Unlike many modern offices, yours is unlikely to have the luxury of air-conditioning to keep you cool in the summer. Working in excessive heat can be unproductive. I experienced this myself when I chose as my first office a south-facing rear bedroom. It had two windows and was a complete sun trap during July and August. It was also not helped by a large amount of office equipment which seemed at one point to have built-in electric heaters, such was the warmth they generated. The following summer, I moved the office to a bedroom at the front of the house which didn't attract the afternoon sun – and was much happier and more productive after making this move. Similarly, another home-worker friend converted his attic into an office, but did not insulate the roof sufficiently. In the summer months, he also found the attic became a heat-trap and only reduced the problem by better insulation.

If you have a large house, which is mostly unoccupied while you work, you may find it more economical to invest in a heater solely for the office, rather than centrally heating the whole house. I do this and also ensure that the window is slightly open to provide fresh air. This is particularly important if you have a lot of office equipment and you can buy an ioniser to help overcome the problems associated with static charges from equipment such as computer screens.

Lastly, if you really want to spoil yourself, air-conditioning units can be purchased which will supply cool air, though they can be expensive to run and many make a noise which could be distracting to yourself and the neighbours.

Lighting

Effective natural and artificial lighting in an office can help productivity and have health benefits. For instance, if you are going to use a computer, you should position screens so that there is the minimum amount of glare either from windows or lamps and especially from direct sunlight. This will help to ensure that you do not get fatigued from poor visibility of your screen. Good lighting is also important if you are doing creative work such as design, photography or artwork and the best type of room light will be natural daylight.

Desktop work surfaces

Desktop work surfaces should be positioned to ensure plenty of natural light while minimising glare on computer screens. My own preference is to avoid work surfaces that face out through windows where you can get distracted, though some people find such distractions comforting. Chapter 10 describes suitable 'healthy' working positions when using a computer, that will help to minimise stress, fatigue and injuries.

New office furniture tends to be expensive and before you splash out, consider visiting one of the many second-hand furniture stores or auctions. It's a sad fact that many businesses fail, but this does have the advantage that there is plenty of second-hand business furniture on the market. Alternatively, if you are good at carpentry or know a reliable local craftsman, you could have some customised work surfaces built, having the advantage that careful design will maximise space.

Positioning office equipment

My own preference for positioning office equipment such as the telephone, fax, answerphone, computer and printer is to have them located within arm's length of my office desk chair. This means that it is easy to pick pages off from the printer and fax without having to get up from the desk chair. The computer keyboard and telephone are also within easy reach, but at the same time, leave plenty of work area. While the computer screen is kept on the desk, the computer itself plus a number of other pieces of equipment, are kept on an adjacent trolley. This is practical as it leaves maximum work surface and makes it easy to get at the equipment for repair or maintenance purposes.

Probably the most important rule to remember is to never let direct sunlight on to equipment, as it could do considerable damage.

STRACHAN CAN TURN YOUR BEDROOM INTO A CONVERTIBLE.

Convert-A-Room is the name of an amazing new home office concept from Strachan, which enables you to turn your bedroom into an office or study (and vice versa) in just 20 seconds, using just one finger.

It is just the kind of innovation you might expect from a company with Strachan's 150 year heritage of fine furniture craftsmanship. James Strachan began as a master woodcarver in 1837 and many of his cabinets, desks and bureaux are now valued antiques. Over the years, the company he founded has supplied fitted studies in timbers such as Oak, Cherry, Maple and Mahogany - combining traditional cabinet making skills with thoroughly modern features including built-in computers, modems and fax machines.

Strachan are the perfect people to turn to, whether you require a luxurious wrap-around office with meeting room facilities or a cost-effective conversion of your under stairs space. Better still, the Strachan design service is entirely free and without obligation.

But not everyone has the space to dedicate an entire room to their home office - and it is with this problem in mind that Strachan developed Convert-A-Room. Concealed beds are housed in cupboards, combined with a swivelling desk arrangement which means that in just 20 seconds your room can be converted from an efficient home office back into a bedroom.

Convert-A-Room is two rooms in one: a space revolution created in response to changing lifestyles and developments such as teleworking. It's another first for the Strachan family of furniture makers.

Why not take advantage of Strachan's free home office planning and design service?

To find out more - and receive a free Convert-A-Room in Action video, phone free now on 0800 212 637.

CONVERT A ROOM
IN JUST 20 SECONDS.

8.20pm it's a study in Maple.

8.21pm it's a bedroom in Maple.

THAT *really is all it takes to turn a fitted study or home office into a beautiful bedroom - thanks to Strachan's unique Convert-A-Room system.*

One finger is all you need to lower your cunningly concealed bed and slide away the desk - and it's just as easy to reverse the process next morning.

Whatever your space restrictions, we can tailor-make the perfect design. And Strachan's reputation for craftsmanship is your guarantee of the highest quality.

There's even a special "Convert-A-Room in Action" video. Take advantage of our Design Service and we'll send you a free copy.

When you see how easy it is to create a study or office in your home - without sacrificing a bedroom - you'll be converted too.

Refreshments

To help you to be self-sufficient in your office, you could keep a small area reserved for refreshments, for instance tea and coffee making. This means that you do not need to go into the rest of the house and possibly be 'pounced' upon by other members of the household when you do not want to be interrupted. If you really want to go to town, you can even install a small kitchen area, complete with hot and cold water supply and a fridge to keep milk and cold drinks.

Storage

It's quite amazing how much paperwork seems to be generated even in a small business. For example, I get inundated with mail-shots of new computer-based products and, like many people, tend to be a hoarder, finding it difficult to throw things away. My two main storage facilities are first, a lot of shelving, and second, two filing cabinets, which have hanging files with plastic attachments for holding the index labels. All these are typical office supplies, available from any good office supplier. It is sensible to have your filing well organised as it really can save time and trouble later when the filing cabinets become full. When this happens it is tempting to buy another cabinet; however, I adopt a filing strategy that when the cabinets are full, I have a clear-out to free up room.

Creating a suitable image for visitors

In the past, most business people would probably not contemplate visiting home-based offices. But many changes are going on in the way people do business these days, with much greater variety and flexibility in the ways that people fulfil jobs. No longer is the home-based business considered as a bit of a joke, with many big corporations actively using 'one-man-bands' and providing employees with home-working opportunities.

Although the tide is turning in favour of home-based offices, this does not mean that visitors will want to 'muck-in' with your domestic arrangements. For instance, if they have to walk through a pile of children's toys, climb a perilously steep set of stairs or negotiate a muddy garden path, this might not set the scene for the start of a harmonious business relationship. Think of the impression visitors will get right from the moment that they enter your property to the time when they are working with you in your office. This is particularly true if the visitor is a potential customer.

As a general rule, it is probably best not to try and hide the fact that your office is in your home, rather, to make a feature of it. For instance, many employees of large corporations like to visit home offices where they can have discussions within a comfortable environment and without enduring interruptions that are commonplace in large offices. Some have less altruistic motivation – if you make the offer, it gives them a chance to have a drink or smoke – habits that are banned in most big companies these days. This can, of course, be a disadvantage, if you dislike these habits. You can 'spoil' your visitors in other ways, for instance by providing high quality coffee and tea – all these little touches help to give an 'individual' impression that is at variance with the rather bland and uniform environment that we have become accustomed to in large offices.

At the same time as providing a comfortable environment, you should also make sure that your office and the route to your office (entrance-way, stairs etc) look clean, tidy and professional. You can take the opportunity to display some of your products, or photographs and other display materials that will provide a good image of your business. If you have visitors regularly, you should provide the appropriate furnishings for the reason they are there. If it is purely for discussion, some comfortable chairs may be appropriate. On the other hand, if your meetings will be taken up by, say, working on artwork, then you should buy a suitable chair for your visitor.

If you do not think that you have the appropriate environment for visitors, there are alternatives. You can visit their offices or meet in other locations, for instance, hotels. These have public areas where you can meet, or private rooms that you can hire. One of my favourite meeting places is the Palm Court Room in the Waldorf Hotel in London, which provides an excellent value afternoon tea – an occasion many of my clients have enjoyed as an alternative to a (more expensive) lunch. If you are a member of a club, meeting rooms are often available, either public or private, such as at the Institute of Directors or the Liberal Club.

Security

Unfortunately, it is a sad fact that we all have to consider protecting our homes from crime. It is of particular importance if you have a home office as once you have been in business for a while, you will be likely to house items of great value. These are not just the obvious items – computers, faxes, printers, portable telephones and so on – but the less obvious, such as company documentation – customer files, accounts, address books, computer data records etc. It is sometimes a useful exercise to think what actions you would need to take if all these items were stolen or damaged. In practice, it could take a long time to recover from such an incident. Indeed, many large companies now spend sizeable sums of money in protecting themselves from such disasters.

Although it is impossible to prevent burglaries, you can take some basic steps to minimise risks. Installing a burglar alarm and security measures such as window and door locks will help to deter the opportunistic burglar. Many different options exist, from the simple infra-red detectors that ring an audible alarm, to those that will automatically ring the police when activated. The local police provide a service of advising on security measures and reputable security companies can be called on to provide quotations for alarms and other measures.

The police usually advise you to mark any valuable equipment with a unique identifying tag that burglars will find difficult to remove. Unless you are unhappy about marking your office equipment, this can help to prevent burglars taking office equipment bearing a label that clearly identifies that the equipment is etched in this way.

Your office address

If you don't like the image your postal address gives, you may like to consider taking a Post Office Box (PO) number – a service provided by the Post Office. They give you a box number, which, together with a postcode, substitutes for your street address. They will then deliver post in the normal way, or you can choose to pick up your post from the local sorting office. This also has the advantage of not advertising your home address which may be important to you if you value your domestic privacy. It also means that if you move home within your local area, you can maintain the same PO box number, despite a change of address.

Where will you put the computer and all the paperwork?

This company based in Canterbury specialises in office furniture and equipment for smaller offices. They often advertise their good value filing cabinets nationally. There is an extensive range of home office computer furniture which makes the very best use of small spaces.

Wise 1 Office Products deliver all over the country and they have a customer service bureau which will answer all your questions on the telephone.

Wise 1 Office Products have the answers . . .

Their catalogue has furniture you won't find elsewhere. If you are stuck for space and looking for something different you must give Wise 1 a ring! They are very helpful.

Wise 1 Office Products, Tel: 01227 781111

3

Legal and financial considerations

Complying with rules and regulations

One of the many reasons why people choose to work from home is that they can escape the bureaucracy that seems to prevent large organisations from acting in an entrepreneurial fashion. If your business is in the services sector where your activities are mostly related to using a single room in your home, where you work with office equipment (telephone, fax, computer, etc) and you mostly go out to meetings, then you are not too likely to be affected by rules and regulations to do with planning, building, noise etc. You can therefore quietly get on with your work without disturbing your neighbours and you are not likely to get bogged down with endless bureaucracy in dealing with regulatory organisations that involve planning, building, health and safety, environmental considerations, fire regulations and so on.

On the other hand, if your home-based business does not fall into this category, you may have to take rules and regulations seriously.

Planning and building laws

In general, if you use less than half the house for business, no planning permission is required. It will be needed if you wish to carry out structural alterations or change the use of your home from domestic to, for instance, office, light industry or warehousing use. Examples of such cases where planning permission should be sought typically involve:

- converting a sizeable proportion of your home into office space for housing employees or part-time workers
- manufacturing products where the manufacturing process gives rise to noise, fumes or smells

Counting the Cost of Crime

Setting up a business from home requires a huge investment in both emotional and financial terms. You wouldn't dream of leaving your home and office uninsured, yet if you were to suffer a theft the costs in terms of lost business and inconvenience would go far beyond solely the financial cost of replacing vital technology and stock. Fortunately you can insure your investments against the risk of crime by installing a monitored Security System to protect your home and possessions.

A lot of burglaries can be prevented. Most are committed by opportunist thieves, and in 2 burglaries out of 10 the thief does not have to force his way in because a door or window has been left open. Burglars like easy opportunities, if they can see a visible burglar alarm they will think twice about approaching that property; furthermore if the alarm is monitored by a company that the burglar recognises they are far more likely to move on to more easy pickings.

Telecom Security are leaders in residential security in the South East, and have been installing monitored alarms approved by the National Approval Council for Security Systems (NACOSS) for over 10 years. As such they are a name well known and respected by their customers and burglars alike! This is because the Telecom Security System doesn't just ring when triggered (as bells probably annoy neighbours more than intruders!) it also alerts their 24 hour fully manned Monitoring Centre who, after checking for false alarms, will notify the Police on your behalf - fast.

A Telecom Security System is also much more than just a very effective burglar alarm. It is a complete protection System for your home and family since it protects them form fire and medical emergencies, and even has the option of gas detection, This protection is via the 3 emergency buttons which are unique to Telecom Security and offer you a direct link to summoning assistance from the fire brigade, police or even your own doctor or the ambulance services.

Truly no other system is a comprehensive in providing you with genuine Peace of Mind Around the Clock. A Security System should be seen as part of your essential business equipment - being without one does not make Commercial sense. See the Telecom Security advert or Freephone 0800 010 999 quoting YHO for your special Reader's Offer and start protecting your home and business today.

- frequent callers, collections and deliveries to your home that cause traffic congestion or road safety problems
- displaying a sign outside your house that advertises your business.

Obtaining planning permission can be a lengthy and costly procedure and you will be well advised to take professional advice from your solicitor to prevent any unwanted attention from local regulatory enforcers. Even if you obtain planning permission, this does not mean that you will be indemnified from neighbours taking future action against you for contravening environmental or health and safety regulations, such as making too much noise or causing road safety problems. Other potential restrictions may arise from:

- byelaws
- listed building restrictions
- conservation area/national park restrictions.

Even if you do not need planning consent for your activities, it still makes great sense to avoid any activities which cause your neighbours annoyance or inconvenience. Defending actions that they or the local authority may bring on their behalf can be costly and time-consuming. Consideration for and sensitivity to your neighbours is a far better approach to establishing good relations and avoiding conflict.

Leases, deeds, tenancy agreements:

It is advisable to check legal documents that relate to the occupancy of your home, for example:

- tenancy agreements
- leases, deeds, charges and covenants
- mortgage agreements.

Such documents can have clauses that forbid the use of domestic premises for any kind of business activity. Again, in practice, if your business mostly relates to using a single room in your home and working purely with office equipment, there is not likely to be too much of a problem.

Insurance

Insurance is one of those annual expenses that most of the time you resent paying, but are thankful for if there is ever a problem. Starting up a home-based business can not only affect your existing domestic insurance, but will also require you to think of some new ones.

Equipment insurance

Most people know someone who has made an insurance claim, only to have it rejected because of some 'small-print' clauses. This is particularly infuriating when you have been paying for a policy for many years in the belief that you are fully covered. The home office worker must beware some 'small-print' clauses to be found in many domestic home contents insurance policies. Not only do these frequently not cover equipment such as computers and faxes that are used for business purposes, but if you have business visitors, you might find that your domestic policy is invalidated.

It is strongly recommended that you let your insurance company know exactly what you are doing and ask them for details of what cover you currently have and what extra you need to pay to cover all your office equipment. It is also important that you get all this in writing rather than from a telephone call where you have no proof of what was said. If your insurance company prevaricates on this issue, it may be better to take out a policy that is specifically targeted at the home-based business. The Federation of Small Businesses (FSB) offers such insurance together with other insurances that are designed for the small business.

When you take out a policy to cover your office equipment you should:

- list all your office equipment, together with purchase price, current value, make, model and serial number
- update your insurance company with any changes, eg newly purchased equipment
- check what sum you will be reimbursed if you make a claim – some policies will pay a replacement value (the cost to replace a stolen item with an equivalent new one) while others will only pay a current value which could be very small in the case of fast-depreciating computers
- read the small print extremely carefully for any 'get-out' clauses
- specify the types of cover you want, such as to cover burglary, accidental damage etc
- decide whether you additionally want all-risks cover for certain items such as portable computers and telephones, enabling you to be covered when you are out and about
- let the insurance company know if you intend to have business visitors
- comply with any requirements for home security measures, such as burglar alarms or marking equipment with unique and unremovable codes.

Dun & Bradstreet

Dun & Bradstreet FREE Directory

Access the details of over 20,000 prospective customers and suppliers...

To give your business a helping hand, Dun & Bradstreet are offering you the chance to win one of our range of Business Registers worth £125 each. Simply fill in the coupon below and post it to us. All entries will be entered into a prize draw which will take place in June 1997, winners will be notified by July 31st 1997 and will win a choice of any one of 30 regional directories.

Businesses by Town & County

Full legal name — **Davidson Motor Spares Ltd.**
Headquarters address — West Hall Road, Lincoln, LU6 2FA
Telephone and fax number — **Tel:** 01522-697453   **Fax:** 01522-697454
Formation date and status of company — **Estd:** 1978 Priv. Ltd. Co.   **Reg. No.** 1469541
US Standard Industrial Classification code and description — **US SIC:** 5013 Automotive parts and supplies
Names and job functions of directors or principles — **Directors:** Mr. F D Davidson (Managing); Mr. P F Stock; Mr. H S P Morrison
Company Secretary's name — **Co. Secretary:** Mr. M P Gibson
Total sales turnover (at date given) — **Sales:** £2,947,362 (31/12/95)
Total Profit/Loss (in brackets) — **Profit/(Loss):** £102,481   **Emp:** 33
Net worth — **Net Worth:** £77,893
Risk Ind: 2
Number of employees / 'risk indicator' / Company registration number

Branch Entry

Full legal name — **Davidson Motor Spares Ltd.**
Branch address — Main St, Grantham, NG31 9YZ
Branch telephone number — **Tel:** 01476-123456
HQ location — **HQ:** Lincoln   **Risk Ind: 2**
'risk indicator'

Businesses by Name

Company name —

AFG Seafoods Ltd.	2
Foster Cars Ltd.	210
Slimfast Clothing Ltd.	496
Wintergreens Ltd.	605

Page number

Businesses by Industry

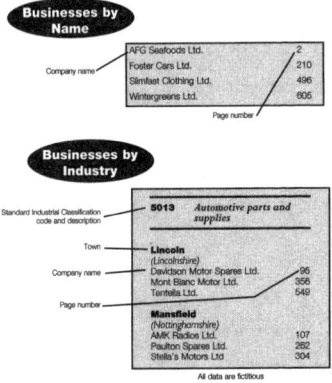

US Standard Industrial Classification code and description —
5013   Automotive parts and supplies
Town — **Lincoln** *(Lincolnshire)*
Company name —
Davidson Motor Spares Ltd.	95
Mont Blanc Motor Ltd.	356
Tentella Ltd.	549
Page number —
Mansfield *(Nottinghamshire)*
AMK Radios Ltd.	107
Paulton Spares Ltd.	262
Stella's Motors Ltd	304

All data are fictitious

- -

Name:

Position:

Company name:

Address:

Postcode:

Tel:

Fax:

Line of business:

Dun & Bradstreet

Number of years in operation:

Number of employees:

Product and public liability insurance

Whatever the type of business you are in, product and public liability insurance will cover you in case you (or your products) cause harm to people or property, be it directly or indirectly. Even if you are purely a home-worker of a large company, you should check whether your employer provides this cover in your home and, if not, take out a policy yourself. This type of insurance will cover you in instances where, for example, visitors fall down your stairs or get an electric shock from a piece of your office equipment or one of your products. It could also cover legal expenses and the cost of complying with enforcements or judgements.

Professional indemnity insurance

In the professional services area, professional indemnity insurance provides a degree of protection against making professional mistakes where you are subsequently sued for damages. Professionals such as accountants, lawyers, doctors, architects and consultants pay an annual fee for such cover and this can cover both yourself and colleagues, provided you supply the insurance company with full details. This is particularly important if you are a sole trader or in a partnership and do not have the protection of limited liability that a limited company provides. In other words, if you are sued as a sole trader or partnership, everything you (and your partners) own can be at risk.

Professional indemnity insurance can be costly and this will depend upon many factors such as your professional experience, qualifications, the area you work in and numbers of employees or partners.

Personal insurances

Although slightly outside the scope of the home office, it is worth mentioning that once you have got settled in your new business, you should consider taking out insurances to help protect against unforeseen circumstance, for instance, if you get ill and cannot work, or to help provide income for your dependants if you die. A pension policy will also provide retirement income in a tax-efficient manner, though the choice of pension plan should take into account unpredictable income patterns that tend to be the characteristic of home-based businesses.

Employer's insurance

If you employ people, employer's liability insurance is compulsory and offers indemnity against liability for death or bodily injury to employees and sub-contractors engaged in the business.

Jury service insurance

While the small business person can attempt to seek exemption from jury service, this will not always be achieved. Jury service can then be severely disruptive and insurance is worth considering.

Car insurance

Check that your car insurance covers you for business as well as domestic use.

Tax implications

Working from home has a limited number of tax benefits. For instance, you will be allowed to claim for a certain proportion of overheads such as heating, lighting and cleaning where it can be demonstrated that these relate to business usage. The calculation will typically be carried out on a basis of the percentage area of floor space that is dedicated to business use. Use of the telephone can also be claimed, though you will need to have a plausible explanation as to the relative expenditure on personal and business calls (itemised bills can help this analysis).

Claiming tax relief on expenses can be a two-edged sword if you own your own property as you may be liable to capital gains tax if you sell your home in the future. However, you can avoid any future capital gains liability provided:

- your home office is not exclusively used for business purposes
- tax relief is only claimed on overhead expenses over and above normal domestic overheads
- tax relief is not claimed on those domestic overheads which do not relate to the business, eg mortgage repayments.

If, however, you rent your home, it will be possible to claim a proportion of the rent that relates to the business usage. In most cases, this will not exceed two-thirds of the total rent.

Unfortunately, the community charge is not a tax-deductible item and, indeed, if it becomes apparent that you are running a business from your home that involves many visitors, collections and deliveries, you may suddenly find yourself presented with business rates on top of your community charge.

Employing people

At some point you may want to take on employees and provide office space for them in your home. While this may appear to be a low-cost option, there are a number of practical, financial and legal drawbacks. First, having a number of employees around can interfere with your domestic arrangements. Second and more important, planning and premises regulations and byelaws are likely to place a range of duties on you to provide and maintain minimum standards of accommodation, such as fire exits and male and female toilets. Your solicitor will advise on your legal obligations. Last, having employees regularly coming to your home and parking outside could be likely to cause annoyance to neighbours. Not only can this cause bad feeling but they may then inform on you if you are not complying with the relevant rules and regulations.

SELF ASSESSMENT

Starting with the 1996/97 tax year, the tax collection system has changed to one of self assessment. Taxpayers, or their agent, are required to compute their own tax liability and make appropriate payments on specified dates. The Inland Revenue will still work out the tax bill if the return is submitted at least four months before the due date. The substitution of a current year basis of assessment for the self employed in place of the preceeding year basis is a necessary part of the arrangement. The PAYE system will remain in place and taxpayers whose only source of income is their salary or wage, will be unaffected.

The first new style returns will be sent out to some 9 million taxpayers in April 1997 and will comprise 8 pages plus 7 schedules although taxpayers with more than one employment during the year, will need to complete schedules for each employment. The return will include a computational section to enable the liability, including capital gains tax, to be calculated. It will need to be completed with figures for all income, capital gains, allowances, reliefs and deductions. It will not be sufficient to endorse sections 'per PAYE' or "see P11D" although employers will be required to provide more information to assist with this.

Frank Ellam, senior partner at Ellam & Company, chartered accountants in Central London, says "Computerising this process has to be the most efficient way of ensuring that no source of income or allowance is overlooked and that the computation is correct". Ellam & Company have invested in the latest systems that can produce facsimile returns acceptable to the Inland Revenue.

Where the taxpayer or his agent opts for computing his own liability, the deadline for submitting returns is 31 January following the end of the tax year. There are automatic penalties for late submission and interest on late payments. The return has to be submitted by 30 September following the end of the tax year if the taxpayer wishes the Inland Revenue to calculate the tax. Frank Ellam believes that most taxpayers will want the advantage of the extra 4 months allowed by including a computation with the return.

Self assessment is not a new tax and does not affect the amount of tax payable. Payment of any tax due will need to be made by 31 January following the end of the tax year although some people, mainly the self employed, will also make two payments on account, based provisionally on the previous year's liability.

It will be the responsibility of the taxpayer to notify the Inland Revenue if they need to complete a tax return or if they commence a new source of income requiring additional schedules. The Inland Revenue will have 12 months in which to ask questions about the figures and will randomly select a number of returns for enquiry. All taxpayers must retain records such as dividend counterfoils and bank statements for 22 months after the end of the related tax year. Business records must be kept for 5 years 10 months after the tax year ends.

Frank Ellam expects that most taxpayers affected by the changes will need help and guidance through the self assessment system and at Ellam & Company they believe in providing a cost effective but personal services to do this.

4

An overview of affordable office equipment

Running a business of whatever size nearly always requires secretarial, accounting and marketing facilities which, in large corporations, are serviced by numerous people, aided to varying extent by technology and external companies. The home-based business, working on limited budgets, has to carry out the majority of these jobs on its own, though they can take up a great deal of time. Fortunately, today's low-cost technology can help with much of the donkey-work, leaving you to get on with your real business. There is an added bonus that, if properly mastered, the technology provides you with greater control and understanding over the business and all its functions.

The key technologies for the majority of businesses are first, the personal computer or PC, which has immense flexibility for tailoring to suit individual business needs and, second, a range of telecommunications devices and services that allows fast, flexible and efficient communications.

The PC has proliferated worldwide and is ever-increasingly to be found in the home as well as in the office. It consists of:

- *a display screen*: on which information (words, numbers, and graphics) can be displayed;
- *a means of storing this information*: either on a removable floppy disc or the (higher storage capacity) hard disc that is located inside the PC casing;
- *the controlling device*: most commonly the keyboard and a pointing device called a mouse;
- *a processor*: the 'brain' that makes it all work.

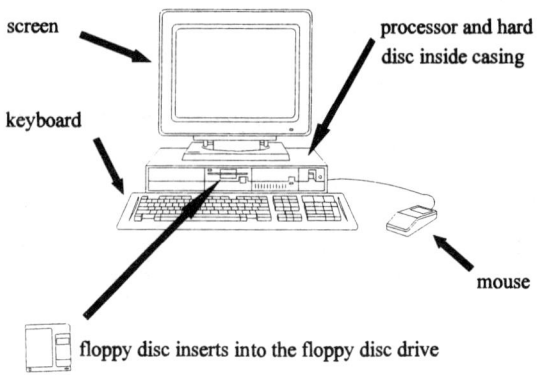

screen

processor and hard disc inside casing

keyboard

mouse

floppy disc inserts into the floppy disc drive

Figure 4.1 *PC hardware*

These components are often referred to as the hardware of the PC (see Figure 4.1).

The PC needs accessories, called software, to make it easy to use; for example word-processing, accounting or desk-top publishing.

Software tells the hardware what to do and provides an 'interface' between the PC and user, to make it easier to use for a particular business need. It does all the complex programming that the computer hardware needs so you only get presented with simple, straightforward and relevant choices, to which you must respond.

Machine	VHS cassette recorder	Personal computer
Information type	Sound & vision	Word, numbers, graphics, sound and video
Storage of information	Cassette tape	Floppy disc, hard disc and CD-ROM
Display of information	TV screen	Computer screen
Control of machine	Push-buttons on machine or remote control	Keyboard or mouse
Machine 'interface'	Record, play-back options	Software

Table 4.1 *Comparison of the PC with a VHS recorder*

Comparison with the video cassette recorder makes a simple analogy (see Table 4.1). The VHS is a machine which displays information (sound and vision) on a TV screen. The information is recorded on to and played back from a removable cassette. But the machine will not record anything until you tell it what to do, so it will give you choices, prompting you to tell it the channel, the week, the day of the week, the start and end time. The complex tasks of controlling the machine are reduced to a small number of choices that are easy to understand – 'record' or 'play-back' – ie, the 'interface'. The VHS will store your choices and record the sound and vision on to the cassette accordingly.

The PC is similar, but a lot more versatile. Instead of a VHS player you have a computer. You are not recording sound and vision, but words, numbers, graphics and even sound and video. Instead of a cassette you have a floppy or hard disc for storing the information and the most recent PCs have a storage device called CD-ROM. The choices of recording and play-back are the simple 'interface' between the machine and person, and is equivalent to the choices provided by computer software. For instance, accounts software will instruct you to type in your sales and purchase figures, your capital expenditure etc and it will then provide you with choices, for example printing invoices, statements, VAT returns, debtors and creditors lists etc.

The choices provided by the VHS cannot be changed – they are built into the machine and are limited to record and play-back; however, you can buy as much software as you like for the PC and load each one into the hard disc from the floppy discs or CD-ROM supplied by the software supplier and use it as and when you need it.

You need only buy software accessories that are relevant to your business. This gives the PC immense flexibility as you can tailor your technology tools to suit your needs. It also means that you can, over a period of time, buy more software to suit expanding business requirements.

This is why the PC is so much easier to use now: the software has been 'fine-tuned' to suit specific jobs and has been designed for the business user and not the computer programmer.

The most critical decision you will make in your choice of technology is your software accessories and these must be chosen to suit your particular requirements. It is far more important to get this right than the computer hardware, which should be selected to match the requirements of your chosen software. Chapter 5 will help you to identify your needs and the software and hardware tools to meet these needs.

Finally, if your business requires you to communicate by letters and reports, for instance, you are a professional consultant, designer or script-writer, it is worth every penny to use a high quality printer. How your letters and reports look will convey lasting impressions to your customers.

Department	Job	Technology tool	Chapter
Secretarial	Letters and reports Standard forms, quotations, paragraphs and reports	Computer and word-processing software	4
	Records of companies and people, eg clients, suppliers Mail-shots	Computer and database software	4
	Message taking, alerting and delivery	Telecommunications services (call diversion, paging, voice messaging) Answerphones, mobile phones, fax	5
Accounts	Bookkeeping, purchase, sales & nominal ledger preparation, stock control VAT returns, debtors & creditors lists, balance sheet Automatic invoices and statements Accounts ready for auditing	Computer and accounts software	6
	Cash flow forecasting and profit & loss prediction Time sheets	Computer and spreadsheet software	6
Marketing	Brochures, letter-headings, business cards Invoices, statements, purchase order forms Colour slides Overhead projector slides Computer slide shows	Computer and word-processing and presentation graphics software combined	7
	Complex brochures	Computer and desk-top publishing software	

Table 4.2 *Summary of technology tools for specific jobs*

Table 4.2 summarises the technology tools that are available and the jobs that they are suited for. There are many more, though only the six most common and useful to the small business have been outlined.

Secretarial tools

The secretary's traditional tool has been the typewriter which has served well for many years. Though typewriters are still an option to be considered, the modern word-processor provides many advantages for the small business as, once mastered, it can dramatically improve productivity.

Word-processing allows you to view the document you have typed in – on the screen. Similarly, you can move chunks of text around and make changes without the need for printing the document or resorting to the Tipp-Ex bottle. You can then store the document and later retrieve it for modification. It will correct bad spelling; help you to choose alternative words with a thesaurus and allow you to store standard letters, paragraphs and forms which can be instantly retrieved and tailored to a particular need, for example, a standard quotation. When the document is finalised on the screen, it can then be printed. It can also print out two or more copies of a document or selected pages, which can enable you to dispense with buying a photocopier (there is still the newsagent's photocopier available, when you really need it).

In addition to the word-processor, you can replace your index cards using a software accessory called a database. This allows you to store details of people and companies in the same way. You can fill in a 'card' on the screen with details such as company name, address, telephone and fax numbers, contacts, a rating of how important they are to you, the industry they are in, how much money a customer has spent with you, and so on.

The database comes into its own when you want to select only certain 'cards'; for instance, you may want a list of all your customers based in London who you have invoiced more than £3000 or a list of all your suppliers who supply engine parts in Birmingham. The database allows such listings to be easily accessible. It is even more useful if you need to automatically send a personalised letter (or it could be a press release) to each one on this list. This can be done by typing out a single letter using the word-processor, leaving gaps for the name, address and 'Dear ....', and the PC will then print out this same letter, automatically addressed to each selected name. It will even print out the address labels as well. This helps you to access targeted customers and suppliers on a regular basis.

A friend of mine runs a small business carrying out contract desk-top publishing for large companies, involving the preparation of high quality technical manuals. He regularly mails both existing and new clients with press releases of contracts won, and new services offered. He gets new company names from various business directories and phones them up to find out the individual he should to write to. *This regular contact will ensure his existing clients never forget him and that he finds new business.*

The PC (at the moment) cannot provide the secretarial service of answering the telephone, though there is a whole range of technologies to help with this. Telephone answering machines are a low-cost option, which even allow you to phone in when you are away from the office and listen to your messages. Alternatively, you could use the new voice messaging facilities offered by British Telecom and Mercury, which act in a similar way to an answerphone, but have the added advantage that they will alert you the minute you receive a message via a small 'bleeper' or 'pager' that you carry with you. You could then instantly reply using a mobile telephone, for instance. Many mobile phones now include such message alerting facilities as a standard feature. Other options available include the ability to divert your telephone calls to another telephone and have three-way telephone conversations.

If you need to get documents to your customers or suppliers faster than posting them, a fax machine will do the job. It will scan the pages (just like operating a photocopier) and copy them via an ordinary telephone line, to another fax machine. It really is like photocopying, except the copy comes out in someone else's office. You can use your existing phone line for this service.

Accounting tools

Bookkeeping has always been one of the dullest chores of the small business; it is mostly done badly and invariably takes up too much of your time, and a sizeable accountant's fee.

If your business involves the processing of a lot of commercial paperwork, it is worth considering purchasing accounts software. It is now very easy to use and can save considerable time and effort. It allows you to type in all your commercial transactions and will automatically prepare your accounts ready for auditing, do your VAT returns and print invoices and statements (generating monthly statements can really help with the cash collection). In addition, you can get print-outs of debtors and creditors and instantly make enquiries on customers: how much is outstanding, what they've purchased and so on. An added bonus is that the VAT and Inland Revenue people are easier to please if they know your accounts are being prepared this way.

Another useful software accessory for accounts functions is the spreadsheet, which can be regarded as the numerical equivalent of the word-processor. Its main use in business is in fast preparation of profit and loss and cash flow predictions to help you plan your business and decide how big an overdraft you will need.

On the screen, the spreadsheet looks like a chessboard – a series of cells. You can type numbers into these cells; you could also type in a formula to add the numerical content of a series of cells together, and it will automatically display the result. The great benefit of the spreadsheet is that if you go back and change one of the original numbers, the spreadsheet will re-calculate the formula you gave it and instantly display the new result.

Expenditure	January	February	March	TOTAL
Mortgage	600	600	600	1,800
Rates	0	0	400	400
Food	120	120	130	370
Drink	35	40	35	110
Petrol	70	60	80	210
Car Insurance	0	500	0	500
Miscellaneous	70	80	90	240
TOTAL	895	1,400	1,335	3,630

Table 4.3 *Predicting household monthly expenditure*

For instance, if you want to calculate your household expenditure you can design a spreadsheet as in Table 4.3. You can break down your expenditure into categories (mortgage, rates etc) and include different figures for each month. The spreadsheet will then automatically calculate the monthly totals for you. If you then decide that your expenditure exceeds your income (when doesn't it?), you can re-think and plan for less expenditure on drink in February or petrol in March (it depends what your priorities are!). The spreadsheet will then automatically re-calculate the totals for you.

You can develop this technique into sophisticated financial models for your business, which will predict your annual profit and loss by calculating your monthly total predicted sales, cost of sales and overheads.

Once you have done this, you can include the formulas to produce a cash-flow projection (for example, collecting cash in 60 days from invoice). It will also help you to estimate exactly what your overdraft requirements are going to be.

Producing a profit and loss and cash flow projection in business is very important. It makes you work out your cash requirements and will invariably demonstrate the need for prompt cash collection and payment control. Most business failures arise from cash-flow problems, where an otherwise effective company went under because they ran out of money, despite on paper having higher invoicing than expenditure! If you are going to need a loan or overdraft, it is much better to be forewarned of this, rather than having to 'fire-fight' when you have the problem. Bank managers are far more likely to have confidence in you (and lend you money) if they see that you have planned your business in detail and present it to them in a simple and readable form.

Marketing tools

Every business has to market its products or services – you have to let people know who you are and what you can do for them. You can do this by using brochures and flyers, by personal contact and by advertisement. How these brochures and flyers look will say a lot about your business. Even your invoice, statement and purchase order forms should look good and be consistent in design. If they are professional looking, your customers are more likely to think that they will get a professional service.

Businesses spend a lot of money on their company identity, particularly the large corporations who employ corporate identity companies to ensure that all their logos, stationery, brochures etc maintain the image they want to portray.

The large corporate identity companies use PCs every day to design letter-headings and brochures – the same PCs that you can have in the home.

The key to creating your professional identity is using your word-processor with a high quality printer to produce superior documents that most people will not be able to distinguish from typeset ones.

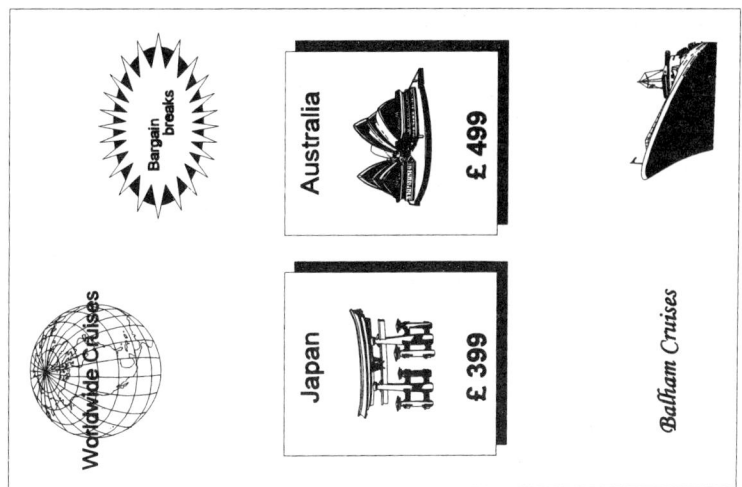

Figure 4.2   *A flyer produced with presentation graphics software*

To give that added 'edge', you can include illustrations, for example, to make a logo. To do this you will need a piece of software called presentation graphics software, which will allow you to draw a logo and include it in your word-processed document. Even if you are not a designer, presentation graphics software has many 'clip-art' drawings for you to choose from and tailor to your need. Figures 4.2 and 4.3 show some examples.

Figure 4.3   *Letter-heading produced with presentation graphics software*

The combination of word-processing and presentation graphics software will allow you to prepare your own professional letter-headings, brochures, with-compliments slips, flyers, forms (invoices, statements, purchase orders) and so on. They can all be printed in your home, without any expensive printing costs. You can prepare the copy for the business cards, but it is probably better to get these printed on a high quality card, at your local printers.

Presentation graphics software has other uses. It also allows you to easily prepare many more types of illustrations, for example charts and graphs. If you are making formal presentations to clients, you can print out on transparent acetate paper, for use in overhead projector slides.

For the office in the home, colour printers have come down in price and are now a realistic proposition, though colour printers that can produce exceptionally high quality documents will strain most home office budgets. Alternatively, you can use a bureau service to make 35mm colour slides or colour prints of your illustrations (you send them a floppy disc containing your illustration and they will send back, by return, your slide or print).

Furthermore, you can use the computer itself to run the illustrations in a 'slide-show', displaying them one after another on the screen, at the touch of a key.

If you are in the design business and need to prepare exceptionally high quality material, eg illustrated brochures and technical manuals, desk-top publishing software provides a tool which will replace the typesetting jobs of the printing world and which will complement the facilities offered by word-processing and presentation graphics software.

5

Choosing your home office equipment

It would be wrong to give the impression that technology tools are going to transform your business overnight into a successful and profitable concern – that is, after all, your responsibility. This book, though, will help you to start the process of using technology tools in a sensible and planned way. The word *process* is used deliberately. While some technology provides a straightforward solution to a particular need, eg the fax machine for despatching documents quickly, others, notably the PC, can meet a wide range of requirements, and the process of identifying and implementing useful solutions requires careful consideration.

The process is relatively straightforward – much the same as when buying a camera or a washing machine – the hard bit is cutting through the techno-speak (that irritates us all) and the large array of possible products. The process means that you have to:

- Find out what's available
- Work out your own needs
- Detail a set of requirements
- Put a realistic plan together
- Buy with confidence
- Learn gradually
- Get yourself organised.

Using this process is rather like learning to swim before you jump in at the deep end. It will demand that you spend more time up-front in getting to grips with technology. Although this is not always easy when starting a new business, the benefits further down the line may well far outweigh your expectations.

Find out what's available

This book will give you a good idea of how technology tools can be useful to you, but a book can only go so far. At the end of the day, *seeing is believing*. Demonstrations of real applications, which match as closely as possible your own requirements, are the best way of appreciating how useful technology tools can be.

So, the big question is – *where do you go to see all this amazing technology?* The first place to go is not a high street shop, unless you want to listen to a salesman who bombards you with techno-speak: 'How many bytes do you want?' or 'You really need much more RAM to run Windows'. This could put you off technology for life. It is far better to go into other small businesses that use technology successfully in everyday situations and visit shops to see demonstrations of the latest technology once you have a better grasp of what you need and what you should be looking for. You probably have many friends and acquaintances whom you can visit to see how they use technology. People are usually only too willing to show off what they are doing and a little bit of flattery will open up all sorts of useful information. At the same time, ask a few pertinent questions. But avoid the technocrats, as they will invariably confuse you, and don't stand for any techno-speak. People often fall into this if they can't answer the question; say 'I know nothing about technology – please keep it simple and non-technical'.

Once your friend or acquaintance is proudly showing their technology tools, be brave and persistent: try some of these questions:

- What are the major benefits? (eg saving money, minimising office administration time, improved customer service and quality, faster communications, enhanced quality in written materials etc)
- What motivated you to start off?
- Did you find it all rather confusing at first?
- How did you learn?
- What problems have you had?
- Where did you go for help?
- How much has it all cost (both in time and money)?
- Would you go about it in a different way now?
- Is the equipment reliable?
- Have you kept up to date with the latest technologies – if so, what would you choose now – and why?

Explain what you are doing and ask advice, but remember it will only be one perspective. Do the same with other people and you will build up a picture of available technologies, their applications and, most importantly, what people have gained from them. At this stage it is inevitable that you will have been given what appears to be conflicting advice. Everyone has their own preferences, thinking that these should apply to others and, all too often, they will focus on the least important issues such as the technicalities; 'You need at least 2 GBytes of hard disc space', or 'You couldn't possibly do without multimedia'. It is far more important to broaden these initial discussions and the technicalities will fall into place once you have identified your business needs and detailed requirements.

Work out your own needs

It is now time to reflect on your own business and be realistic about your real needs. It is likely that you can think of uses for all the technology tools you have seen but it is unlikely that your budgets will allow you to buy everything. It is best to keep to the rule of only using a particular technology tool if the investment in its purchase and the time spent mastering it is likely to pay off with a significant benefit. For instance, if you run a small professional consultancy with only a small number of monthly invoices and few purchases, do you really need a sophisticated accounts software package? In the same way, if your business is providing a car driving tutoring service, do you really need a fax machine when most of your customers are unlikely to have one – even though it might be a nice toy to own. *Learn to differentiate between toys and tools.*

Table 5.1 lists a selection of different home-based businesses. In each category one or more particular needs have been identified where technology could be of benefit. For instance, an antiques retailer could minimise his administration time and costs by using an accounts software package that allows stock items to be kept, purchases and sales recorded and accounting information to be prepared – VAT returns, debtors and creditors lists, sales analysis, profitability assessment etc.

Now, the retailer could do all this manually in books – or pass it on to an expensive accountant. Doing it himself will not only be cheaper but will also free up time for doing what he needs to be doing – buying and selling antiques. Good accounts software will also provide valuable information on the most profitable areas of the business and help in budgeting and cash flow prediction. Furthermore, if bookkeeping and

Business	Principal Needs	Jobs	Tools
Professional Consultancy: management; information technology; safety; quality; technical; design	Efficient preparation of written materials - maintaining a highly professional image to clients	Quality proposals, letters, reports, brochures, presentation material	Word-processing and presentation graphics software with high quality printing
	Fast and efficient two-way communications with clients	Message taking, alerting and delivery	Answerphone; fax; mobile phone; call diversion; paging
	Keeping clients, press and suppliers informed of your business successes	Maintaining register of clients, press and suppliers and sending regular mail-shots and press releases	Database software linked to word-processing (and presentation graphics software)
	Minimising office administration time	Accounting, business planning and project management	Accounts, spreadsheet and project management software
Writing: Journalism; book-writing; script-writing	Maximise time available for writing - with fast up-dates to written material	Efficient production and revision of written materials	Word-processing software
	Response to tight deadlines and two-way communications	Fast delivery/receipt of written materials and message taking	Answerphone, fax and electronic mail
	Access to information databases	Locating specific information from newspapers, journals etc which are electronically stored	Either (1) information retrieval software linked to CD-ROM discs or (2) on-line information services linked via a modem and communications software
	Minimising office administration time	Bookkeeping, VAT returns, accounting, accounts information	Accounts software

Business	Principal Needs	Jobs	Tools
Legal: Solicitor's advice	Efficient preparation of written materials - maintaining a highly professional image to clients	Quality letters, affidavits etc. Retrieval of standard paragraphs, clauses etc	Word-processing software.
	Access to information databases	Locating specific information on past cases etc	Information retrieval software linked to either (1) CD-ROM databases or (2) modem-linked on-line information services
	Response to tight deadlines and two-way communications	Fast delivery/receipt of written materials and message taking	Answerphone, fax and electronic mail
	Minimising office administration time	Bookkeeping, VAT returns, accounting, accounting information	Accounts software
Home Services: Cleaning; gardening; catering; upholstering; piano tuning; play groups; picture framing; window cleaning; catering	High quality written materials	Brochure, catalogue and price list preparation	Word-processing and presentation graphics software
	Ensuring customers are always answered	Message taking	Answerphone
	Minimising office administration.	Bookkeeping, purchase, sales and nominal ledger preparation, stock control, VAT returns, debtors and creditors lists, balance sheet, invoicing, statements	Accounts software
	Regular promotion of business services to new and existing customers	Maintaining register of existing and potential customers and sending regular promotional material	Database software linked to word-processing and presentation graphics software

Business	Principal Needs	Jobs	Tools
Car services: Repair; servicing; radio fitting	Minimising office administration	Bookkeeping, purchase, sales and nominal ledger preparation, stock control, VAT returns, debtors and creditors lists, balance sheet, invoicing, statements	Accounts software
	Ensuring customers are always answered and responded to quickly	Message taking and diverting	Answerphone, mobile telephone and pager
Media and Communications: PR; advertising; marketing; corporate identity; design; market research; photography	Efficient preparation of written materials - maintaining a highly professional image to clients	Quality proposals, letters, reports, brochures, presentation materials	Word-processing, presentation graphics and desk-top publishing software with high quality printing.
	Fast and efficient two-way communication with all clients, suppliers, press and other contacts	Message taking, alerting and delivery.	Answerphone, fax, mobile phone, paging, call diversion.
	Keeping clients, press and suppliers informed of your business success	Maintaining register of clients, press and suppliers and sending regular mail-shots and press releases	Database software linked to word-processing (and presentation graphics) software
	Minimising office administration time	Accounting (bookkeeping, VAT etc), business planning and project management	Accounts, spreadsheet and project management software.

Business	Principal Needs	Jobs	Tools
Financial services: Accounting & book-keeping; financial advice; auditing	Maximise available working time and providing fast, accurate response.	Book-keeping, purchase, sales and nominal ledge preparation, stock control, VAT returns, debtors and creditors lists, balance sheet, invoicing, statements, business planning etc	Accounts and spreadsheet software
	Presenting a highly professional image.	Quality letters, reports, proposals	Word-processing software with high quality printing.
Basic office services: Typing; telephone answering;	Maximise available working time	Quality letters, reports	Word-processing software
	Fast communications	Efficient telephone answering, faxing, message taking	Answerphone, fax, mobile phone, paging
Advanced office services: Typing; (Type-setting; presentation materials	Maximising available working time, fast response, in-house control and quality output	Preparation of quality reports, graphics, flyers, brochures, slides	Desk-top publishing, word-processing and presentation graphics software with high quality printing
	Fast transmission of written materials	Electronic transfer of data to clients and printers	Modem and communications software
	Minimising time spent on office administration	Book-keeping, purchase, sales and nominal ledger preparation, VAT returns, debtors and creditors, balance sheet, invoicing, statements.	Accounts software
	Fast and efficient two-way communications	Efficient telephone answering, faxing, message taking, alerting and delivery	Answerphone, fax, mobile phone, paging, call diversion

Business	Principal Needs	Jobs	Tools
Retailing: Antiques, jewellery, market stalls, Tupperware, home furnishings	Maximise time available for selling, buying, manufacturing	Full accounting facilities - book keeping, purchase, sales and nominal ledger preparation, stock control, VAT returns, debtors and creditors lists, balance sheet, invoicing, statements, business planning	Accounts and spreadsheet software
	High quality written materials	Quality product lists, brochures, letters, presentation material	Word-processing and presentation graphics software with high quality printing
	Ensuring customers are always answered	Message taking	Answerphone
Personal services: Teaching, tutoring, clothes making, hairdressing, manicuring, photography	Present a highly professional and quality image to clients in written materials	Quality written materials	Word-processing software
	Ensuring customers are always answered	Message taking	Answerphone

Table 5.1 *Identifying needs*

For the office at home, here's the solution: no office.

In the world of home computing, the Apple Macintosh Performa range is designed to make life easier — whether you're working, playing, learning or communicating.

And by combining the right hardware with the right software, there are now complete computing packages to suit your specific needs.

The Apple Home Office package is designed for people who work from home — a high performance PowerPC based Macintosh Performa complete with Claris-Works, ClarisImpact and Claris Organiser. It will let you create business presentations,

manage your diary and accounts, and keep track of your customers.

It's Internet-ready and with Apple Telecom software, will also turn your computer into a fax, a telephone and an answering machine. So whether you run your business from home or simply bring work home from time to time, all the office space you need is a corner of your desk.

Call the Apple Information Centre on: 0800 234 800 for further information and details of a Macintosh Performa stockist near you. Alternatively, you can fill in the coupon.

Please send me more details about the Macintosh Performa range and stockists near me.

Mr/Mrs/Ms/Other _____

First name _____

Surname _____

Address _____

_____

_____ Postcode _____

Daytime Tel _____

I would like a stockist to contact me to arrange a demonstration ☐

Return to: Apple Information Centre, FREEPOST, London SW15 2YY. HSDE1

Apple

HOME SWEET HOME

GESIKA

OFFICE FURNITURE

In the past people had to leave their homes to be able to take advantage of the benefits linked with the use of the new technologies in place at factories and offices. Nowadays, these same technologies make it possible for people to be linked to the business world and enjoy the same benefits from the comfort of their own homes. On-line systems, e-mail, the internet, multimedia etc. give the office at home a real opportunity to succeed in today's business world. At the same time the office at home helps reduce environmental problems such as congestion in town areas. It is also economically viable as it helps companies and individuals to reduce the amount of rent to be paid for office space.

Due to the above circumstances there is an increasing number of people who either like to work from home, have to work from home or are allowed to work from home. In some cases, part of a room which is normally lived in is used for this purpose. Therefore, it is of great importance to have a comfortable place to work from which blends into the domestic environment.

GESIKA LIM, following the principle Less Is More addresses this problem by combining peoples' leisure and working life in an optional way. Its design puts an emphasis on simplicity, clarity and joy of life: Table legs made of slender rounded tubes, together with a seemingly floating desk top, create a grateful environment.

GESIKA LIM is adaptable to any type of situation. If, for example, guests are expected after work, the desk can be converted easily into a dining table without looking out of place. Even the pedestals can serve as occasional tables, thus creating a comfortable environment for an enjoyable evening.

LIM offers a complete range of functional, practical, flexible and technically advanced workstations. Pedestals, credenzas, cupboards and wardrobes in three different heights and four different widths complement the GESIKA home office programme. Thus, GESIKA is in a position to provide cost effective solutions to meet everybody's needs. Maximising space with the best options available is the main philosophy of this programme.

THEEXPRESS

 NEW Titles from The Express series

THE EXPRESS

NEW **Titles from The Express series**

The Express Investment Guide
Practical Advice for Making the Right Choice
Second Edition
Tony Levene

Do you find the choice of investment options now on offer bewildering? Do you want some impartial, clear advice on the pros and cons of the various alternatives available? If so then **The Express Investment Guide** is for you.

Well informed and jargon free, this guide covers the full range of investment choices for individuals, looking at everything from building societies and banks to the stock market. Essential for anyone wanting to save or invest a sum, however large or small.

£7.99 Paperback ISBN 0 7494 2015 4
128 pages March 1997

The Express Guide to Buying a Property Abroad
A Practical Guide for Overseas Homebuyers
Second Edition
Niki Chesworth

Do you dream of living abroad? Whether as a second home or a permanent residence, more and more people are turning such a dream into reality. Written in a clear, down-to-earth style **The Express Guide to Buying a Property Abroad** pinpoints the common pitfalls that can make the dream a nightmare. Every area is covered, including:

♦ a detailed country-by-country guide
♦ a thorough assessment of all the costs and benefits of moving
♦ a discussion of the different ways of buying

£7.99 Paperback ISBN 0 7494 2017 0
184 pages March 1997

Available from all good book shops or to obtain further information please contact the publishers at the address below:

Kogan Page Ltd
Pentonville Road, London N1 9JN
Tel: 0171 278 0433, Fax: 0171 837 6348

Competitive price

Maximum

performance

The Maxiputer

CTX's ultimate computer system, integrating home and office features into a single communication centre. Fully interactive entertainment and education features, in an all-in-one, convenient, space saving and easy to use package, that offers it all.

Monitors

CTX monitors are renowned for excellence in the computing industry with highly acclaimed 17" monitors and award winning multimedia monitors CTX offers the widest choice of the highest quality and best priced monitors in the market.

Notebooks

'*What PC?*' nominated the EzBook *gold* for best budget Notebook 1996 and now the introduction of the new CTX CyberNote offers the ultimate high end notebook performance.

LCD Projectors

Connect the EzPro 500 up to your PC - instant large screen presentations, connect up your video - instant large screen TV or cinema. The ultimate light and bright projector.

LCD Monitors

The Panoview range represents a totally new concept in visual displays and are ideal for laboratory panels, point of sale, banking, military and medical applications.

CTX Europe Limited

7 Woodshots Meadow
Croxley Centre
Watford
Herts WD1 8YT

Tel: 01923 810800
Fax: 01923 818643

CTX

OFFICIAL SPONSORS OF WATFORD FOOTBALL CLUB

COMPUTER PRODUCTS

THE ✠ EXPRESS

New and best-selling titles in The Express series

Now established as sound reliable sources of advice on money matters, The Express Guides show anyone how to:

◆ make the most of their money

◆ get a business venture off the ground

◆ know their legal rights

Available from all good book shops or to obtain further information please contact the publishers at this address:

Kogan Page Ltd
Pentonville Road
London N1 9JN
Tel: 0171 278 0433
Fax: 0171 837 6348

Creating an office at home, whether as a support for a regular place of work or as the basis for your own entrepreneurial venture, can be an immensely rewarding and exciting undertaking, but it is not without its pitfalls.

Not everyone is cut out to work on their own. Working from home requires self-discipline, self-motivation and the willingness to stick at any job until it's done.

Small Business Solutions

A reliable method of keeping in touch with customers, suppliers and business contacts is vital for any home office and a mobile phone can be a particularly useful tool when you work on your own own. In some cases in fact, a mobile phone is a viable alternative to installing a second phone line into your house. And, with a mobile phone as your business line, you enjoy the added benefit of being able to take your business phone with you when you have to be away from the office.

Alternative to a fixed-line phone

One 2 One customer Sebastian Smith uses a studio in Covent Garden as the principal base

for his graphic design business, Imperial Digital. However, because Sebastian is a sole-trader, he often finds himself bringing work home at night and on the weekends.

He used to have fixed-line pho as the main contact number for t design business. However, becau he was dividing his time between Covent Garden and home offices well as spending several hours week visiting suppliers and clien Sebastian was missing calls an subsequently, business opportuniti

To ensure that he always receiv his calls, Sebastian replaced the fixe line phone with the One 2 O mobile phone service.

One 2 One
communicatio
for self-s

"With my mobile as my on business phone, wherever I g Imperial Digital goes with me a my clients only have to rememb one number. Ultimately, this mean can provide better customer servic he said.

Because all One 2 One servi packages come with **free VoiceMa** not only does Sebastian not miss call, the dozens of messages he g each week are absolutely free retrieve.

One 2 One's peak and off-peak c rates are among the lowest in the l industry and local weekend calls a free of charge with most One 2 O service packages, so Smith has fou his One 2 One phone is a viable alt tive to a fixed-line office phone.

bile Fax and Data Services
eates an office to go

e Sebastian, Internet Consultant
chard Conway wanted to be his
vn boss. Mobile fax and data
vices from One 2 One have made
possible for Richard to set-up
obal Media Communications in
s north London home using a
ptop computer, a data card and
okia 2146 mobile phone connected
the One 2 One data service.

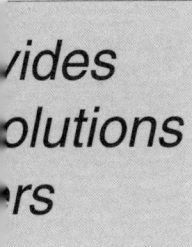

Because all
the tools of his
trade are por-
table, Richard
can now con-
duct his busi-
ness at his
home office or
anywhere in

e One 2 One's coverage area –
rrently 80 percent of the GB
pulation – the same as if he were at
office in the City using a desktop
and a regular telephone line.

"I have a great deal of flexibility
th my work," said Richard. "I can
ave my home office to visit clients
d feel confident that I can send a
x or an e-mail or even design a Web
e, any time I want to."

Before One 2 One launched data
rvices early in 1996, Richard was
d down to his desktop computer,
xed-line phone and modem to
rform everyday business activities
ch as sending and receiving e-mail,
ding faxes, retrieving information
om the Internet and transmitting

data files to clients and associates
throughout the world.

One 2 One offers subscribers data
calls at a cost as low as 12p per
minute day or night, among the
lowest rates in the industry.

"Because the One 2 One service is
high-capacity it is more reliable than
other mobile data services that I've
tried in the past so I don't experience dropped calls or difficulty
getting through to a destination
whether on a voice or data call," said
Richard.

Many Extras

With a reliable VoiceMail service and
the Gold Service Package's
memorable number option, Global
Media Communications also has a
professional image.

When working from his north
London home office, Richard also
takes advantage of the Gold service's
Inside Option which enables the
customer to nominate an area or
address and receive further discounts
on mobile phone calls made from
that address, with calls costing as
little as 3.5p a minute.

Rapidly Expanding Coverage

More businesses can take advantage
of One 2 One's high-capacity digital
phone service as it reaches 80 percent
coverage of the GB population by the
end of 1996, and 95% by the end of
1997.

For more information about One 2
One, call 0500 500 121 and quote
reference PR 1853.

**(All prices include VAT at 17.5 per
cent)**

IF YOU are setting up an office in your home, Danka can meet all your Home Office needs.

From a full range of colour and black and white copiers, printers, and fax machines to the most responsive service in the industry, Danka is *the* single source solution.

On September 9, 1996 Danka Business Systems and Kodak Office Imaging agreed to join forces worldwide. This merger will make Danka the strongest independent provider of office imaging products in the world, with over 22,000 employees and 700 offices in 35 countries.

This merger offers Danka customers more options than ever before and as the strongest independent suppliers of photo-copying and facsimile units in the world, Danka are committed to making office equipment the most reliable part of any business.

So, whether your requirements are large or small Danka can help you to make the right choice.

Danka – World Class Products, World Class Service at your fingertips.

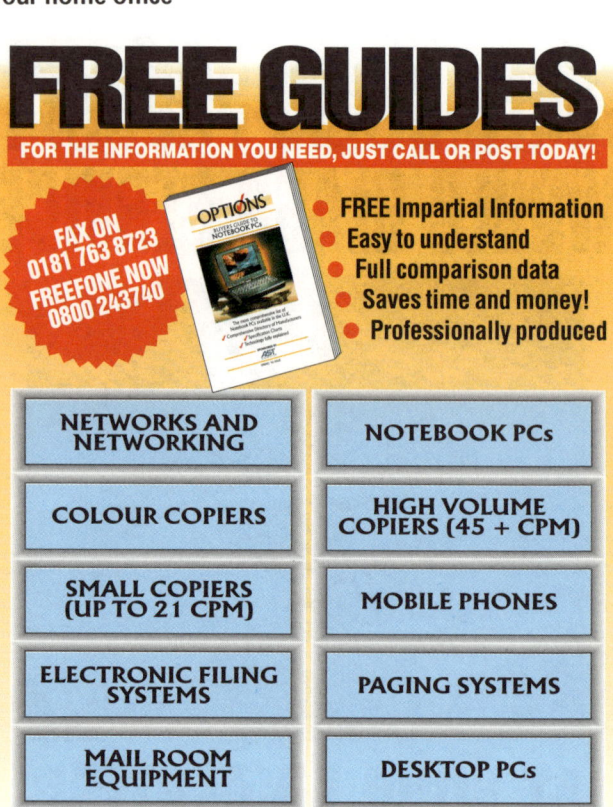

accounting intimidate you, you may well find that accounts software can help you to overcome your fears – it can be a great way to teach yourself how these practices work.

Having compared your business with those in Table 5.1 does not mean you should rush out and buy all the suggestions for technology tools. You should only invest where there is justification. Remember, all the listed jobs can be bought in, for instance, if your faxing requirements are likely to be infrequent, then a local faxing service is an option. However, if you require these services frequently, you should seriously consider acquiring tools to do them yourself. Owning these tools will also allow you to have greater control over the quality of your work and enable you to provide faster response to your customers – without the dependence on other businesses. Don't overlook this advantage; it is this kind of service that the small business gains over large, more bureaucratic organisations. If you are regularly sending out mail-shots to many customers it will help to build up your own database of customers; that way your investment in collecting names and addresses and putting them into the computer will have the pay-off that you can send regular mail-shots when you like, with minimal cost.

A scriptwriter friend reckons that since she started using word-processing software for script preparation, instead of her local typing service, she is able to turn out three times the quantity of work. As her scripts frequently require rewriting, the advantage of the word-processor over the typewriter comes into play – even though she is not a touch-typist (she maintains that she can type as fast as the words come to her mind).

The 'principal needs' listed in Table 5.1 also emphasise the quality of written and presentation materials. Remember, in many home-based businesses, it is likely that much of your contact with customers will be via written materials, from which they will develop an image of your company. It is important that you take time and trouble to convey the right image, which will also help to overcome many people's prejudices about home-based businesses.

Large corporations pay large sums of money to corporate identity companies who advise on how the corporation can convey the right image to the outside world. You too can create your own company identity by churning out highly polished written materials, complete with drawings and illustrations.

Your business may or may not come into one of the categories in Table 5.1. Either way, it is useful to write down a similar table yourself, identifying your business, principal needs, jobs and technology tools. Do a separate section for each need and leave space for detailed requirements.

Detail a set of requirements

Whenever you buy any major item – a house, car or camera – the buying process is always simplified if you spend time detailing your exact requirements. Remember, when you walk into a shop, the assistant knows nothing about you or your needs. The more information you can supply, the more likely they are going to be able to help you. Think of the house-buying process. Similarly, you would, in one way or another, prepare a very detailed specification, such as location, price range, closeness to regular transport, number of rooms, condition, size of rooms, type of house, heating system and so on. When you do this it can save wasted time looking at unsuitable properties – estate agents permitting.

Take each sheet where you have listed a principal need and now fill in your detailed requirements. Some likely issues are listed below:

Fax

- Number of faxes per week (if you are going to be a heavy user of a fax machine, buy one that will stand the strain)
- Using the fax as a photocopier (many will do this, though the quality is not too good: does this matter to you?)
- Single or multiple sheet feeding (if you are going to send large documents, don't buy one that can only take five sheets in the sheet-feeder)
- Using the fax as a printer to a computer
- Portability (if you are travelling a lot, a portable fax machine may suit you: though remember, if you take it with you, you leave the office without one)
- Fax and answerphone combined (enabling a single telephone line to be used both for phone calls and faxes)
- Automatic paper cutter
- Grey scale as well as black and white (important if sending, for instance, photographs)
- Stored regularly used numbers (it all helps the office efficiency)
- Printing on thermal paper (where the writing deteriorates with time) or plain paper sheets.

Answerphone

- Remote access (phoning in from outside the office to pick up messages)
- Recording conversations (in case your memory fails you; it can't be done secretly though – the answerphone will sound a beep to your caller to alert them that the conversation is being recorded)
- Dictation facility (saves buying a dictating machine).

Telephones

- Touch-tone phone (necessary for the new BT/Mercury services)
- Telephone hands-free operation
- Stored numbers (regularly used numbers stored in the telephone)
- Mercury facility
- Display of telephone number for incoming calls
- Portable/mobile phones.

Mobile phones

- Size and weight
- Battery requirements
- Geographic coverage
- Tariffing options
- Operation in a car.

British Telecom/Mercury services

- Number of telephone lines
- Separate line for fax
- Call diversion (diverting calls to another telephone, eg a mobile telephone)
- Call interrupt (having two calls on a single telephone line)
- Three-way calls (enabling three-way conversations)
- Itemised billing (to identify business and private calls and check bills)
- Call barring (facility to block certain types of call, eg international calls)
- Voice messaging (like an answerphone)
- Cheap long-distance and international calls (eg via Mercury, cable TV services)
- Free local calls (eg using certain mobile phones or cable TV telephone services).

Paging

- Type of message (eg bleep or text message on a small display)
- Linked to telephone and voice messaging.

Computer

- Amount of storage space (will depend on the software you choose and the quantity of information you need to store)
- Desk-top or portable (and battery operation)
- If portable, size and weight; quality of screen; size/weight of transformer; battery life, ability to connect a larger screen and keyboard
- Amount of memory (will depend on the software you choose)
- Computer standard (eg IBM, Apple)
- Expandability (what peripherals you can connect)
- Up-gradeability (eg increase in speed, higher storage and memory)
- Ease of use
- Compatibility with chosen software and hardware
- Speed of operation.

Printing

- Quality of printing
- Speed
- Graphics printing
- Portability
- Colour printing
- Overhead projection slide printing
- Envelope printing
- Sticky label printing
- Choice of fonts
- Compatibility with chosen computer and software.

Computer modem

- Speed
- Built-in or external to the computer
- Inclusive of a faxing facility
- Compatibility with communications software and computer.

Word-processing software

- Ease of use
- Sophistication
- Different language capability
- Spell checking, thesaurus and grammar checking
- Graphics capability
- Screen appearance (whether what is displayed on the screen is identical to how it will be printed)
- Automatic indexing, contents page generation
- Mail merge
- Columns/tables/spreadsheets
- Compatibility with computer and printer
- Compatibility with presentation graphics software
- Compatibility with your customers' or colleagues' software.

Presentation graphics software

- Compatibility with word-processing
- Compatibility with computer and printer
- Range of fonts
- Ease of use
- Range of clipart.

Desktop publishing software

- Ease of use
- Range of fonts
- Flexibility to lay out text and graphics
- Compatibility with word-processing and presentation graphics software
- Compatibility with computer and printer
- Compatibility with printing bureaux.

Spreadsheet software

- Ease of use
- Printing flexibility
- Graphics features
- Compatibility with computer and printer
- Compatibility with word-processing and accounts software.

Database software

- Compatibility with word-processing and spreadsheet software
- Mail-merge capability with word-processor
- Compatibility with computer and printer
- Ease of use.

Accounts software

- Sales ledger
- Purchase ledger
- Nominal ledger
- Stock control
- Bill of materials
- VAT returns
- Reporting (eg debtors, creditors lists)
- Balance sheets
- Numbers of different transactions
- Automatic invoicing and statements
- Ease of use
- Compatibility with computer and printer
- Compatibility with your accountant's software.

Communications software

- Compatibility with computer and modem
- Ability to connect with different electronic information services
- Ease of use
- Electronic mail facility.

Computer utilities

- Hardware and software tools to help organise, protect and back-up your information.

Electronic information services

- On-line services or on CD-ROM
- Range of information services.

Photocopier

- Numbers of sheets per week
- Colour capability
- Speed
- Range of paper sizes (eg A4, A3).

Miscellaneous issues

- Security of access to computer
- Warranty period
- The necessary accessories and extras to get everything working
- Quality of manuals
- On-site maintenance
- Delivery times
- 'Hot-line' telephone support services, particularly for computer hardware and software.

Costs

- Purchasing/leasing costs
- Operational costs (eg toner/ribbons for printers, floppy discs for the computer, call charges – particularly for mobile phones)
- Maintenance costs (either returning to supplier or on-site)
- Likely repair costs
- Delivery costs.

An example of putting together a detailed set of requirements is given for the case of two women (Anne and Ethel) who have set up a comedy scriptwriting team (see Figure 5.1 and Table 5.2) and use technology to make it realistic to work from home.

As well as identifying what technology tools you need, it is just as important to realise what you don't need. In Anne's case, she does not like accounts, but sees the need for doing her own bookkeeping. She uses a simple accounts package to do this, leaving the tax and more complicated accounts work to her accountant. Furthermore, though a mobile telephone would be useful to her on occasions, she cannot justify the high cost of the phone, its rental and call charges – preferring to have a BT charge card facility.

Anne is a famous comedy scriptwriter (so she tells me) and works in a team with Ethel – both from their own homes. When she first started writing, she used a local typing service when sending material into the TV companies. This typically cost £50 per script and, with many rewrites, could total over £200 per job. It was also slow having to wait for the typing company to do the work.

Now she uses a computer, word-processor and printer. She bought a second-hand computer from a company that went into liquidation, together with a laser printer, and bought word-processing software via mail order. She also has a portable computer which allows her to work in France, where she has a home, and in the USA. She has a fax machine, also bought from the firm in liquidation and has recently purchased a low-cost bookkeeping accounts package.

Anne reckons that having the word-processor enables her to do three times the amount of work compared to her old method of using a typing service. But she is more positive about the role of the technology. To her, it is more than just a typewriter. Her writing style has evolved with the word-processor, so that she 'thinks' with it and it has helped her to become a better writer. Anne cannot type very fast, but she finds this is not important as she can type as fast as she thinks things out.

Her writing partner, Ethel, also has the same computer and they have recently each bought a modem and communications software for their PCs so that they can transfer the word-processed files to each other using telephone lines. In this way, they can both work on the same script without having to be in the same location. They can also both now access the Internet and use it to send files to each other.

Anne now has a new lifestyle and freedom to be able to work in different countries and at times to suit her. Because it has increased her efficiency so much, she has probably become successful more quickly than if she did not have the technology tools.

Anne first became interested in computers when she bought one of the Amstrad word-processing machines and that gave her the idea of using word-processing. She has progressed to using a simple bookkeeping and accounts package and this forces her to keep her books in order and help prepare her VAT returns quickly. She finds that the VAT and Inland Revenue people are happier when the accounts are computerised and she even saves a few hundred pounds on her accountant's charges.

Anne spent £1,100 (second-hand) on the computer and laser printer in 1994 – an Elonex 486, with 340 MByte hard disc. She uses Microsoft Word (for Windows) word-processing software (cost £240) and Money Manager accounts software (cost £50).

Figure 5.1 *Anne and Ethel's comedy scriptwriting business – Anne's detailed requirements*

Business	Principal needs	Jobs	Tools
Script-writer	Maximise time available for writing, with fast up-dates to written materials and minimising administration time	Efficient production and revision of written materials and simple bookkeeping	Computer, word-processing software, simple accounts software, printer
Detailed requirements	**Computer:** large storage capacity, portability, IBM standard, compatibility with word-processing and accounts software, ease of use **Word-processing software:** ease of use, French, American and UK language capability, spell checking, thesaurus, automatic indexing, contents page generation, columns, compatibility with computer and printer; different style formats for scripts (speech and directions) **Accounts software:** simple bookkeeping, ease of use **Printer:** high quality fast printing, different font capability		
Business	Principal need	Jobs	Tools
Script-writer	Response to tight deadlines and two-way communications	Fast delivery/receipt of written materials	Answerphone, fax, modem, communications software
Detailed requirements	**Answerphone:** remote access (phoning in from France and USA) to pick messages up **BT/Mercury services:** Diverting calls and faxes to home in France; cheaper international calls; telephone charge card **Fax:** combined with answerphone on single telephone line **Electronic mail:** modem and communications software for exchanging word-processed files; access to the Internet **Miscellaneous:** low-cost A4 photocopier; utilities software for organising, protecting and backing-up information; on-site maintenance; hot-line telephone support for hardware and software (that operates internationally)		

Table 5.2   *Anne and Ethel's comedy scriptwriting business – detailed requirements*

Put a realistic plan together

Having reached the stage of identifying your needs, it would be unwise to rush out on a 'spend, spend, spend' buying spree. It is doubtful whether most home-based business start-up budgets would even allow this! It is also a good idea to take one step at a time – learn and master one tool before moving on to the next.

So prioritise your needs. What are the most immediate? It could be that the most important is to have a telephone answering machine to take messages while you are away from the office. Other tools such as a fax can wait until you have sufficient cash available (after all, if you look hard enough, you can often find a nearby shop, office or friend who can send and receive faxes for you temporarily). These machines are relatively easy to buy and the time spent in buying and learning them will not be too great.

You may well have decided that your business needs dictate buying computer tools. The great thing about computers is that you can buy software packages in stages, according to your plan. For instance, you could buy word-processing software initially and then your accounts software later. Having said that, it is still a good idea to work out your overall needs first as the choice of one software package may well influence the choice of another, in order to be compatible. For instance, if you require a word-processing facility and need to be able to mail-shot large numbers of customers on a regular basis, then you should buy word-processing and database software that are compatible with each other. One option is to buy packaged software that combines a number of different individual and compatible software items, such as word-processing, database and spreadsheet in a single package, though they usually sacrifice flexibility and feature range for compatibility purposes.

When putting the plan together, also be realistic about time spent on buying and learning about your tools. This can take much longer than you think.

Buy with confidence

If you've followed the steps above so far you are on the right track to buying with confidence. You will know what you want and what it needs to do. But the next stage is just as important as it is here that you will begin to home in on the most suitable products for your purposes. You may well know that you want word-processing with ten particular features, but now you have to choose the particular product. It is a good idea to get some advice when deciding to buy and there are a number of options, ranging from asking friends and acquaintances to using consultants or your local high street shop.

If you know a friend or acquaintance whose opinion you can trust, you can probably get good advice for little expenditure. But beware, *treat technocrats with caution!* The more technical someone is, often the less business oriented they are and they will tend to go for 'toys' rather than tools. They also invariably fail to understand the position of someone who does not communicate in techno-speak and often end up causing more confusion than when they started.

Consultants are listed in *Yellow Pages* and there are organisations that provide consultancy services (such as the National Computing Centre) which are independent of computer hardware and software companies, though it is advisable to ask them for customer testimonials. But think carefully before using a consultant; after all they are not always as independent as you think and can be expensive. They are just as interested in selling more of their services to you and if you're not careful their bills will start to follow the spiralling prices that we have come to expect from the legal profession. Even if you are using a consultant, still go through the process described earlier in determining your needs.

As with any professional service, the better you brief the professional, the better their advice can be. Ask the consultant for a fixed price fee quotation for a given detailed scope of work. Both parties then know exactly what is being provided and this saves possible disputes later on. For instance, you might just want a couple of hours' advice to confirm the choices you have made. Alternatively, you may want the consultant to write a detailed product specification for you to go and buy yourself or, you may want them to do it all for you – including buying, installing, getting it all up and running for you and training you how to use it. In some cases, such as if you are too busy with work, this might be appropriate – but you will pay a lot more and it does have the disadvantage that you could become dependent upon their expertise. It is far better to take control of your own technology, as this builds confidence and in the long run you will be better off from doing it yourself.

Another option is to go into a computer shop and buy a complete service, asking them to specify, install, get it up and running etc. This is an advantageous option if you are short of time, though it can also be expensive and you should be aware that such advice is rarely independent. Advice usually only extends to the products that they happen to sell and there may be a tendency to over-sell. The other day I went into a London shop to enquire into a combined fax and telephone answering machine, asking what was the cheapest on the market. They dutifully demonstrated one for £350, which they confirmed was the cheapest on the market. When it was pointed out to them that there was an alternative for £200 two shops away, they admitted that they did not stock that brand and what they really meant was that the £350 model was the cheapest *they* sold. This is a good technique to use when buying. Ask a few questions that you know the answers to, as this establishes whether the sales assistants are being 'economical with the truth' or are giving any old reply when they don't really know the answer.

If you have the time, though, choose your products yourself. This part of the process all adds to the learning curve and the more you know, the more confident you will be. You can also have fun doing it. In fact, it is quite a good idea to treat this part of the process as entertainment. Remember the comedy sketch on TV many years back – the hi-fi sketch – where a man plays a thoroughly untechnically minded buyer going into a hi-fi shop to buy a 'gramophone', and gets bombarded with questions like 'How many watts?', 'Do you want a woofer?', 'Would you prefer an equaliser?' and so on. The same intimidation goes on in computer shops. Assistants will try to intimidate you with techno-speak to put you on the defensive and it is often a cover up for ignorance – so that you won't ask them difficult questions.

But don't let this put you off. Turn this around to your advantage. Here are some useful tricks:

Read up

Before venturing into shops, buy several different magazines (see Chapter 14, Additional information) to get an idea of prices. If you are a newcomer to the technology world, you will find some of these magazines confusing as many of them assume a certain technical knowledge. However, there are some extremely useful sections in them, such as features on best buys for laser printers, portable computers, accounts software and so on, together with comparisons of different brands.

Play dumb

Once you venture into a shop, play dumber than you are – that way you will be able to test how genuine and knowledgeable the sales assistant is.

No techno-speak

Ask the sales assistant to stick to plain English – and any time they lapse, just remind them that you do not speak their language.

Get everything explained

If you do not understand anything at all, demand an explanation in plain English.

Ask simple questions

The simpler the question, the harder it is to answer, for example, 'Is this particular word-processor fully compatible in every way with the printer and computer you recommend?' But make sure that you delve into the reply in some detail to check that a confirmation has not been given out of ignorance.

Get it demonstrated

Ideally, you should ask to see a demonstration of the equipment you want in exactly the configuration you intend to use it. However, in practice you will find that this is not always possible, particularly when it comes to different software packages running on different computers and printers. The sheer number of permutations and combinations sometimes makes this unrealistic for shops to demonstrate. But you should get a written guarantee stating that the different components you intend to buy are fully compatible with each other and, if they are not, you will get a full cash refund. This tends to focus their minds!

This philosophy, however, should not apply to accounts software as the complexity requires some very detailed understanding of what it does and how it will integrate into your business.

Have a look at the manuals

The manuals are going to be very important to you. Without a manual that you can understand you will be using your equipment 'blind'. Ask to see them.

Have a go yourself

When it comes to software, if you have a particular feature that is critical to your needs, you must spend time playing with it yourself to check whether it does what it says it will. This is particularly true for complex accounts software, where it is often not possible to ascertain its suitability until you have spent time using it.

Shop around

Go into a number of shops to get different views, perspectives and quotes and play one off against another; for instance, if the second shop recommends a different product from the first and their choice is more expensive, tell them what you can get more cheaply and ask them to justify their decision. Then go back to the first shop and do the same. This can help getting to the nitty gritty of things! It also builds up your knowledge and puts the sales people on the defensive!

If you feel confident that you know exactly what you want, you can buy direct using mail order. The best deals are possible this way, though don't expect the best of telephone expert advice either pre- or post-sale. Some computer magazines provide a mail order protection scheme which takes away some of the risks of this particular buying method. And beware of buying from abroad, as you may find that you will not be able to get any help or maintenance for the product in this country.

Avoid impulse buying

It can be very easy to get carried away in a shop and agree to something you might later regret. Sales people are trained in getting customers to do this! It is usually a good idea to reflect on things overnight, before committing yourself.

What is included in the price

Check what is and what isn't included in the price:

- Will they deliver free of charge?
- Will they install and get it fully working free of charge (and in the case of computers, with all software fully working together)?
- What is the returns policy for damaged or non-working equipment?
- What period is the warranty (remember you are protected by the Sale of Goods Act)?
- Is on-site maintenance provided? If so, which company carries this out?
- What will be the on-site maintenance charge in two or three years' time?
- Is the product the latest version? If not, a discount should be given
- If on-site maintenance is included, what will be the call-out time when there are problems?
- Are all cables, plugs and batteries included?
- Are floppy discs included in the price?

- Are printer ribbons and toner included?
- What do new printer ribbons, ink or toner cost and how often will they need replacement?
- Is VAT included?
- Does the computer come with floppy discs and CD-ROMs that will enable all the software to be re-installed if there is a problem?
- Are all the manuals included in the price?

Who you buy from

Be careful when choosing what brands you buy and where you buy from. There are numerous companies around and a good few of these do not have a stable financial structure. It is not always easy to decide which are the most secure (both small and large companies can go down the pan) but generally speaking, it is best to buy from the most well-known companies.

Negotiate

If you have followed advice, you will have a good idea of what you need and how much it is likely to cost, but use the powers of negotiation. Give the sales assistant the impression that you are being talked into something you actually want and always make comparisons with quotations from other shops. If you are buying a number of items, it is often possible to negotiate a good discount, or at least one or two small extra items thrown in.

Placing the order

Once you are satisfied that you have a good deal, make sure of the following:

- You have a fully detailed, itemised, dated and signed quotation which covers all the included items (including delivery date).
- The quotation should also state that all the items you have bought will be fully compatible with each other.
- Better to pay by credit card if possible as there can be a degree of protection if the supplier goes bust.
- Only pay the full amount once you have received the goods.
- The quotation should state the period in which, if something goes wrong, you will get a replacement, rather than a repair (put in writing).
- If you have to sign a delivery note and it states 'received in working order' cross this out and put 'received but not operated yet'.

One other buying option is to go for second-hand equipment. This can save money, though it is possible that the equipment is either in bad condition, out of date, does not have a maintenance contract or the owner, who has spent a lot of money on it, cannot accept that computer equipment depreciation is faster than for cars and will not let it go for a cheap price. Having said all that, if you can buy something really cheaply, it may be worth it – it can get you started for minimal price – but it is probably better to buy from someone you know and trust. I know a company who were sold an outdated computer (second-hand) for little money; however, the cost of running it, buying software and the annual maintenance contract was much higher than had they bought new.

Learn gradually

This is the exciting bit – the new 'toy' has arrived and with great anticipation, it can be unwrapped. A word of caution, though; do read the instructions for putting it together and starting it up. It can save you endless frustration and there are often necessary safety and practical precautions to observe. And don't forget to return the registration forms. For some products, particularly computer software, this will be necessary when you ring them up for help (it's their protection against software piracy) and help lines can be extremely useful.

Computer instruction manuals are gradually getting better. They often come divided into sections with a short one to get you going, such as 'Getting Started Quickly' and a more detailed one, such as the 'Reference Manual' for when you have mastered the basics. This helps with getting something to happen quickly without having to read a long manual. For example, if you have bought a fax machine you probably want to send a fax to a friend straight away and if you've just taken delivery of a PC, word-processor and printer – you will want to write and print something quickly.

Reading and understanding the manuals will be the only way to fully learn your system. Now, this does not mean that you should sit down and slog through a 500-page manual in one go (yes they can be as long as this). Rather, you should learn the basics first and get things to happen – this gives confidence. Then take a typical everyday need and read up about it in the manual. For instance, using the word-processor to check the spelling of a letter.

From then on, learning is a mixture of finding out as your needs dictate and scanning through the manuals to learn new features of the technology tool. For instance, having written, printed and checked the spelling of a letter, you may want to use the thesaurus of the word-processor to give you ideas for alternative words. In so doing, you may discover a feature to allow you to sort lists into alphabetical order.

Though manuals have improved over the years, there are now many excellent books available that deal with the well-known computer software products – geared to varying levels of ability – and it is worth looking at a number of these to see if they can complement your manuals.

If you are short of time, you may find it useful to go on a short training course. Many organisations run these, for example, local firms and universities. A friend of mine, Eric, recently took a two-day training course at his local college in the use of PageMaker desktop publishing software. It cost £225 all in and he reckons it was money well spent. It taught all the basics and provided hands-on experience under expert tuition, together with additional training manuals. He is considering returning later in the year for a course on advanced uses of the package.

Magazines devoted to the PC (see Chapter 14, Additional information) can also be of help in learning, providing features on getting better use out of particular software products and readers' problems.

It can also be worth while joining a user group such as the IBM PC User Group.

And don't forget the telephone hot-line services that you get with computer hardware and software. These, like manuals, are getting better and better and some now operate on a 24-hour basis.

Get yourself organised

One of the most important things to do once you've got over the initial elation period of your new equipment is to make sure you are well organised. If, for instance, you have bought a fax machine, remember that paper runs out and can take a while to order. Be organised and make sure you always have a spare roll handy.

Storing information on a computer, eg word-processed or accounts information, requires more attention to organisation than is needed by a simple fax machine. As you use the computer more and more, the information that builds up will become more valuable to you and there will be a lot more of it than when you first started. Just as you spend time on filing paper in cabinets and keeping detailed bookkeeping records, computerised information requires the same thoroughness in referencing, indexing, backing up and categorising. And to do this you

Eric provides the music industry with writing, journalism, design and printing services. The final 'product' may simply be a press release, or it could be a corporate newsletter or company brochure.

Up to 1990, Eric used mainly fax and telephone answering machines, with a switching device that enables both machines to use a single telephone line. The fax allows his clients to speedily send their requirements and allows him to reply with suggestions for press releases, articles, newsletters etc. Speed is of the essence as his clients invariably take too long in making their minds up in giving him the order and are then unreasonable in demanding instant attention (we all have empathy with this but remember - fast service is one of the plus points of the small business).

At the same time, he was using an Amstrad word-processor to type his copy. However, the type-setting was prepared using external companies, with associated delivery delays, and he would then manually paste up on a drawing board. The process was generally expensive, slow and made him dependent on other companies.

In 1990 he purchased an Apple computer and laser printer with desk-top publishing, graphics presentation and word-processing software which now provides him with the facility of being able to typeset all material in his own office and in 1994 he updated his equipment with a new Apple computer. He can lay out everything on the screen and draft it on to the printer. The quality is good enough for many applications, although for some professionally finished material (eg company newsletters and brochures) he has the final version printed using a bureau printing service - it is a simple process to send the data file on a floppy disc to the printing bureau, where they will then print what is called a bromide. Any colour or black-and-white photos are inserted on to the bromide and this is then ready for bulk printing.

The advantages to Eric's business are many. He is not dependent upon outside companies; it is much cheaper; he has control over quality; he can visualise how things will look and, more importantly, show the customer how it will finally look before it is too late to make changes. He has increased his turn-around of work and can now respond much more quickly to his customer (particularly important for press releases).

Except for his experience on the Amstrad word-processor, Eric had no prior knowledge of computers and did not like the thought of using them. In order to learn, he went on a two-day training programme run by the local polytechnic. He found this extremely helpful in showing him the basics of the desk-top publishing software, and giving him hands-on experience, under expert guidance.

His next step is to purchase a modem so as to be able to send his data to the print bureau over the telephone lines - saving even more time. He also wants to buy a scanner, in order to be able to scan photographs into the Apple.

He purchased an Apple Mac SE2, Apple Laserwriter II laser printer and a Taxan Viking A3 monitor (he needs a large monitor to help lay out) and has since updated the computer with an Apple Mac LC475. He uses PageMaker, Quark Express and MacWrite software and bought the hardware second hand from a company for £2500 (the company sold the equipment as they found, to their cost, that having the equipment does not make a designer out of a technocrat!). He uses a PanaFax UF150 fax machine, and finds the local shop's photocopier economical to use. He regards a mobile phone as a waste of money.

Figure 5.2 *Eric's writing and design company*

must read the manuals to fully understand how your computer works and how it stores and retrieves information. Think of the computer as a filing cabinet and start to organise the storing of your information in separate directories, folders or sections.

Backing up information is far more important than people realise. A sudden power cut can cause misery if it results in the loss of a valuable document or last month's bookkeeping records, making you realise how dependent you can become on your PC. I would like to think that you will always act on this recommendation, but have learnt that even when saying this to clients or friends, they still make the same mistake of under-estimating the importance of backing up. So I'm not going to preach any more – find out the hard way yourself!

How much it will all cost

Go into a photographic shop and say 'I want to buy a camera – how much will it cost?' and it is unlikely that you will be given a price until the sales assistant has helped you to work out what you want. Camera prices can start at £40, though you could end up spending well over £1000. It's just the same when buying technology, except the options are far greater and the price range is much wider.

One aim of this book is to help you narrow down those options and to identify the tools which will help you to run your business efficiently, rather than helping you to buy 'toys' – gimmicks that look good but don't do a lot for you. To help you get a rough idea of prices, each section of the book that describes a particular technology provides a range of typical non-VAT prices.

The prices given are only a guide to early-1997 values to help you with a broad idea of what to expect, but technology prices have a tendency to change rapidly (mostly downwards, though this trend may not always continue). When implementing the buying process described in this chapter, you should carry out your own survey of prices to get the most up to date.

Overcoming techno-fear

The technology industry has, in the past, done its best to confuse people – designing products that are hard to use, products that can supposedly do all things for all purposes. It has even invented its own jargon to intimidate people into buying what they do not need and produces instruction books that require a degree in computer science to make sense of.

Furthermore, we have all experienced the company computer department which perpetuates the myth that *only* they should control technology, and where their (misguided) motivations stem more from job preservation than for the good of the company. No wonder people are reluctant to fork out hard-earned cash on technology when the industry has not made it easy for them.

This confusion induces 'techno-fear'. But remember, it is a fear that others have created. *And it can be overcome.* It requires approaching technology on the same basis as you would your business – being methodical about choosing what you need, what you buy, how you master all its features and how you use it.

Knowledge and understanding will lead to confidence. And confidence is the key to overcoming techno-fear – in the same way that an effective saleswoman, who knows her product inside out and what it will do for her customer, will be a confident saleswoman.

Finding out is time well spent

There is an almost overwhelming number of technology products and brands to choose from, often with a multitude of features and with varying levels of flexibility and ease of use. When deciding what you need, don't rely on one person's advice. Talk to a number of people and go into a number of shops to get demonstrations. Asking obvious questions, which are usually the most difficult to answer, will test the salesperson's knowledge. Product reviews in magazines can be extremely helpful in the decision-making process and they often provide comparisons between different brands, albeit with a tendency to focus on technical merit rather than on the customers' real needs. Get as many opinions as possible and thoroughly explore what is available. This will help you to decide what the market-place has to offer and what is best suited to you.

Do you really need it?

Deciding whether you really need a technology tool is the most important decision you will make – preferably before you go out to buy! For instance, if your business is a professional consultancy, your main requirements will probably be to print high-quality documents (your letters and reports are your 'product') and to enable effective communication (possibly with answerphone, fax and electronic mail), though sophisticated accounting tools would probably not be a requirement as the number of commercial transactions are relatively small. However, if your business involves selling products in quantity and there are many invoices and purchase orders, the primary requirement will probably be for a bookkeeping and accounts tool.

Don't fall for the jargon

Salespeople have targets to meet and are often paid on a commission basis, so it is in their interests to sell you more than you need. A well tried and tested method is to bombard you with technical jargon which will either send you rushing out of the door or intimidate you into buying more. If they start talking in techno-speak and you don't understand, stop them and ask for a simpler explanation, or try saying 'I know nothing about the subject – please describe it in layman's terms'. Give them your problem and ask what they think. Play one off against another and use the routine 'but the shop down the road said this product would be more suitable'. Get them to justify their suggestions.

Don't pass the buck

It's all too easy to cop out of getting to grips with technology and ask someone else to set it up and get it going for you (children will be only too glad to oblige). You will never gain confidence this way. It might take a little longer, but having done it once, you will know what plugs into what and how it all works. So when someone else accidentally pulls a wire out or changes the settings, you'll know exactly what to do. *Do it yourself.*

Get something to happen

Once you have installed your technology, don't try to run before you walk. Do basic things first and certainly don't try to read the entire manual as this will probably put you off for life. Manuals usually have a 'getting started' section which will allow you to gain early confidence with simple operations before trying the more advanced features. For instance, if you have decided to invest in a word-processor for your PC, as an alternative to a typewriter, try typing a short paragraph, filing it and printing it out – there's nothing like actually producing a printed document to give you a good kick-start, and the more advanced features, such as spell-checker and thesaurus, can be discovered later.

Learn from your mistakes

When my father was teaching me to drive, he would let me practise putting the car into skids on snow or ice, to help gain confidence in controlling it under any weather conditions. The same rule should apply to learning how to use technology. Never be afraid to try different things. Knowing your technology inside out will lead to confidence in use and, fortunately, the impact of getting it wrong is a lot less severe than if a car skid goes wrong! *You can afford to make mistakes.*

It's more indestructible than you think

Over the past ten years, I have carted all sorts of different technology tools (including PCs) around the world, on trains and planes, and have even had a PC dropped from a crane on an oil platform. So far, there have been no failures and, though my own experience is perhaps not universal, most people find modern technology to be extremely reliable – even surviving small children in schools!

When the going gets tough

It would be misleading to paint a picture that all will be a bed of roses. There will be times when you want to chuck your computer or fax machine out of the window because you can't work out how to do something. It is all too easy to lose motivation. Make a basic rule: don't think of other things to do when the going gets tough. Use the available help features, such as reference manuals, the manufacturer's telephone hot-line facility or help from the shop where you made the purchase.

Learning

Many technology tools, such as answerphones, have a limited range of features and these can be learnt from the manuals. However, the PC has immense flexibility in providing many different and sophisticated tools, many of which you may never need, and it may well be prudent to take a course to make you aware of the extent of the features and to master those that you need. Learning from instruction books is an alternative, but the cost of the course may well be saved in your time trying to teach yourself!

Keyboard skills for your PC

One of the great things about the PC is that you don't need to be a touch typist to use it proficiently. The companies who design applications for the PC realise that people frequently make mistakes and they design their applications to expect this. However, it is worth becoming familiar with the keyboard and to practise your typing techniques. This will save you frustration. After all, would you be confident of driving a car without really being able to control it? You don't necessarily have to invest in a typing course, though this is a fast way to learn. There are plenty of good books that are widely available and it is even possible to buy typing training courses that use your PC to train you in typing skills.

6

Be your own secretary

You may be asking, 'Can technology replace all the job functions of a secretary?' The answer is – not all. There are many jobs, such as going to the post, buying stationery, binding reports, that all mount up in time and which people have often taken for granted in companies. However, it is swings and roundabouts; the time you lose on these jobs is counterbalanced in other ways, such as not having to travel to work (for many people, this can be two hours a day wasted) and not having to attend unproductive office meetings.

But there are plenty of technology tools that will help you to perform many of the functions of a good secretary. Most of them are software packages for your PC, that allow you to prepare high-quality letters and reports, quotations etc, and to keep records of companies and people. The two key elements are word-processing and database software packages and this chapter describes what they do and how they can be used. The technology tools that can be used for the other main function of a secretary, that of message taking, are described in Chapter 7.

But you may say that using a word-processor requires a skilled typist and it is an inefficient use of time if you don't have that skill. In the days of typewriters, this may have been true; however, the word-processor can make doing it yourself highly efficient, as it is much more than an alternative to the typewriter. It can help you to formulate and develop ideas and can even help to cultivate your thought and working processes. It allows instant access to everything that you have ever written, enabling the material to be used again and again, adapted and modified for different needs and without the need for retyping. You can also include drawings and illustrations in documents, to help explain points clearly.

The efficiency gains from doing it yourself far outweigh the benefits of someone else typing, where you may have to proof-read several versions, correct mistakes and be at the mercy of their time-keeping.

The big secret to achieving efficiency is organisation and thorough knowledge of your technology tools. At a basic level, you have to ensure that there are adequate supplies of stationery, ink for the printer, paper for the fax etc, so that you do not run out at the wrong time. Of equal importance is the need to get to grips with how each of your tools works and to gain experience so that you know how they work under different situations. It's rather like riding a powerful motor-bike. The experienced rider can race it to its limit – the slightest flick of the wrist and the bike responds instantly – an extension almost to the rider's well-trained mind and body. Think of technology tools as an extension to your mind and body, allowing you to 'ride' extremely fast through a day's business with extreme efficiency and effectiveness.

Recently, another consultant joined my network of consultants. He was used to having a number of support staff in his last company and it took him quite some time to get used to doing all the secretarial tasks himself. He found that attention to the small details was the most difficult and frequently typed letters with incorrect names, addresses and telephone numbers. He wasn't bothering to check them as, in the past, there was always someone to do this for him.

It takes time to learn and adapt technology to suit your own way of working and requires refining your attitude towards doing your own secretarial work – which is more than just doing the typing. You will need to develop the characteristics of a good secretary:

- Efficiency
- Organisation
- Attention to detail
- Learning the tools of your trade
- Self-discipline
- Quality of work.

The word-processor is much more than a clever typewriter

As a general rule, and like with all general rules there will be many exceptions, for every ten features in a technology product, possibly only one is actually used. This applies both in the home (do you use all the features on your video recorder?) and in the office. Though some manufacturers are to blame for this – providing products and manuals that are difficult to understand – it is often the case that people do not consider that word-processors can do a lot more for them than their typewriters can. Because of this, they do not bother to learn what the advanced features can do and how they can be of potential benefit.

The word-processor can be used not only for reports, letters, notes, faxes, electronic mail, invoices and brochures, but can also link with other software, such as databases, for carrying out mail-shots, and with presentation graphics software, for the inclusion of drawings and illustrations in documents.

Word-processing basics

In case you are not aware of what word-processing can do, first of all an explanation. Word-processing software can be bought to operate on your PC and comes in a pack that contains floppy discs (or a CD-ROM) which store the software. A set of manuals will usually include instructions on how to run this software either off the floppy discs themselves, or, more likely, how to transfer the software on to the hard disc of your computer and then operate it.

When you give the command to start the software, it will load it into the computer's memory. You can then type something on to the screen of the computer. A small cursor on the screen, that can be moved around either using the up/down/left/right arrow keys on the keyboard or the mouse, allows you to type text anywhere on the screen. You can then insert new text or over-write what you have already typed. At this stage, everything you have typed is still in the computer memory, which will lose it when you turn the computer off, unless you store what you have written either on the hard disc or a floppy disc. You can do this by giving the document a unique file name. This means that, at a later date, the file can be retrieved using this unique file name. You can also print the document on your printer.

At first appearance, this may not seem too different from a type-writer; however, some really important advantages begin to emerge:

- You don't have to be a really good typist – you can make mistakes as you are typing on to the screen and then go back later and correct them without having to waste paper and time.
- Document drafts can be printed and checked; the original file can then be easily corrected and the final version quickly reprinted. This is where the word-processor really scores over the typewriter.
- The spell-checker will check for misspellings, even giving suggestions for words that you might have intended.

- Chunks of text can be moved about into different sections of a document. This is particularly useful when preparing large documents, such as a report or book, as you can do the easy sections first and leave the most difficult until last.
- Standard text that you type frequently can be stored permanently and instantly retrieved and modified to suit different needs, saving retyping each time (such as storing a brochure 'template' of text for tailoring to individual customers or industries).
- The thesaurus can suggest alternative words.
- The print quality can be extremely high, depending upon the printer you use. You can choose from many different fonts (or type-style), text size and shape, in order to give a high quality finish to a document.

When you've mastered the basics of word-processing

As with learning to drive a car, it is important to be comfortable with the basic handling before moving on to more advanced techniques. The same is true with word-processing. Do not be too adventurous at first until you understand the basics, such as:

- How to name and store documents
- How to organise and find them (particularly when you begin to amass a large number)
- How to edit, delete and insert text
- How to move blocks of text around.

Then you can go on to discover the more advanced features of the word-processor:

- Different types of printed output can be selected, for example, A4 paper, envelopes, labels (for envelopes), acetate paper (for overhead projection slides);
- Searching and replacing text; for instance, if you have a standard brochure with one of your customers' names frequently included, you can instruct the word-processor to replace all the entries of this customer's name with a new one;
- Documents can include automatic page numbering (with different positions for odd and even pages);
- On certain laser printers, the word-processor can print on both sides of the page at the same time;
- Headers and footers can be included (for instance document and chapter titles alternating on odd and even pages);

- Footnotes can be included and automatically numbered;
- Different fonts, styles and sizes can be selected;
- Text can be positioned in different ways – lines can be left, right, centred or fully justified and different margins selected;
- Text can be put into column mode, in a similar manner to newspapers. This is particularly useful for brochures or articles;
- Tables can be included; many examples of such tables are found in this book and it all helps in presenting information clearly;
- In long documents, headings can be marked so that the contents page can automatically be generated (complete with page numbers). This is particularly useful when preparing drafts of documents which undergo many revisions – the changes will automatically update the new contents page;
- A separate index can be created at the end of a document, complete with page numbers, by marking individual words in the text;
- Cross references can be made in a document, say to a particular page (eg, see page 4), where if the page numbering is changed, the references are automatically updated to reflect the correct page number. This same facility applies to references to figures, drawings, paragraphs etc;
- Standard forms can be prepared without the need for having the forms especially typeset and printed, for example quotation forms;
- Letter headings can automatically be generated using special type-styles and graphics – saving the need for having letter headings typeset and printed;
- The word-processor can 'learn' combinations of key-strokes and allow those same combinations to be easily repeated by pressing a single key; this can provide a useful short-cut facility when preparing complex documents;
- Standard styles of written material can be remembered by the word-processor, for example report styles with particular fonts and font sizes – enabling each style to be quickly retrieved for a particular need.

Word-processing price range
£30 – £250

Some word-processing software can be bought as an integrated package which comes with spreadsheet, presentation graphics and database capabilities, though stand-alone word-processing software often includes an ability to integrate with other stand-alone software. Either way, such facilities provide some powerful tools:

- Drawings and illustrations can be created using presentation graphics software and then included in a word-processed document, positioned wherever you like in the document;
- Word-processors and databases can be linked together to provide what is commonly called a mail-merge facility; this allows you to prepare a single letter that you may want to send to a large number of people. All you do is type the letter and insert special codes where you want the name and address to be inserted; you then select the individual people from your database and instruct the word-processor to create the same letter each time – personalised to the individual names and addresses. In the same way you can also print the envelopes or sticky labels for the envelopes;
- Information on a spreadsheet can be included in a word-processed document, for instance, if you are preparing a proposal to the bank manager, you can include figures from the spreadsheet within the body of the text;
- If you use desktop publishing software for preparing highly polished print material, it can sometimes be more efficient to prepare much of the text using a word-processor. The desktop publishing software can then access this text automatically.

Integrated software price range
(word-processor, spreadsheet, database, graphics presentation)
£80 – £300

You don't need speed typing

The versatility of the word-processor excuses both slow and inaccurate typing and provides one of the key advantages over the typewriter. Whereas a good typist could be a company's valuable asset to efficiency and productivity, now the technology has bred a nation of mediocre typists. Unless you are a purist, this can only be a good thing. It allows all of us to use word-processing.

This means that fast typing speeds are not essential. After all, it is not as though you are mindlessly typing someone else's work – it is your own and you have to think it out as you go along. However, when you first start to use word-processing, it is tempting to write things out in long hand and then type them in. It is far better to avoid this stage and progress straight to typing directly – you will soon begin to see the advantages.

Having stated that typing expertise is not essential, the better your typing, the more easily you will be able to use your word-processor. There are a number of books which can help you to learn correct typing techniques – where to place the fingers etc – and there are also computer-based training software packages available, which will take you through training exercises to develop fast and accurate typing skills. If you are a complete novice to the keyboard, you won't have any bad typing habits to shake off and you can learn the correct technique from square one. What's more, if you really want to get off to a good start, how about taking a touch-typing course? You wouldn't regret it!

Computer-based training for typing
£50 – £100

Using a database as an electronic card index

As your business builds up, you will begin to amass many contacts – customers, suppliers, press, general contacts, etc. Now you could keep lists either on an ordinary card index, or you could use your word-processor. In many cases, a listing on a word-processor might well be appropriate; you can use the word-processor to sort the list into alphabetical order and the key-word search capability can be used to locate specific people or company names. It is also very easy to update the list with new entries and revisions. Separate pages can also be used for different categories, eg customers or press.

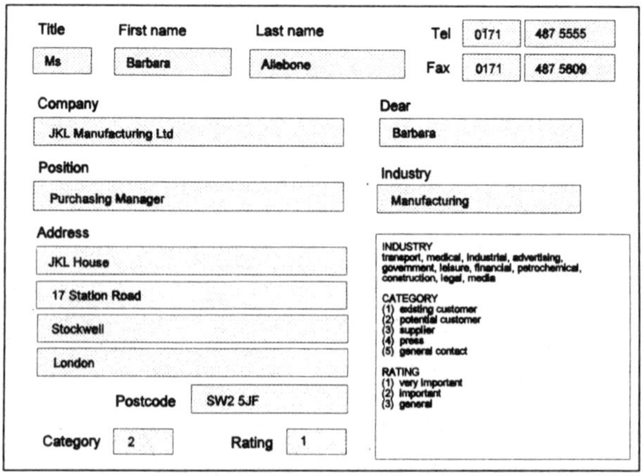

Figure 6.1 *Typical database template*

However, there can be many advantages in using another software program – the database – to store your information. The database allows you to build an electronic card index of people and companies. It does this by letting you specify a template of individual pieces of information that you want to hold – just as you would with an ordinary card index – containing various relevant details about a company, such as your contact name, their position in the company and the telephone and fax numbers. This 'card' or 'record' as it is called in database terminology, can then be filled in for every contact that you have. Figure 6.1 illustrates such a (filled-in) template. As well as the basic items (name, address, etc), additional information can be included to help when carrying out mail-shots for selected people and companies. Figure 6.1 includes individual items of information such as:

- **Dear**
  This item decides what gets printed at the beginning of a personalised letter *(Dear ...)* in a mail-shot. If you know the person well, you can use their first name *(eg Barbara)* or if you wish to be more formal, you can use their title and last name *(eg Ms Allebone)*.

- **Category**
  By categorising your contacts with a code, you could then easily identify them, for instance, *1* for existing customers, *2* for potential customers, *3* for suppliers, *4* for press.

- **Rating**
  You could rate your contacts with a code to identify how important they are to you, eg *1* for very important, *2* for important, *3* for general.

- **Industry**
  You could specify the industry your contact works in, eg *medical or petrochemical.*

When you come to set up your own database template, you have the flexibility to specify the various information items that are relevant to you. As an example, you might prefer to have information concerning a company's turnover, its number of employees and its product range included in the template.

Once you have filled in the details of all your contacts (this does take some time), that is where the worth of the database comes into its own. You can search the database and ask it to print out a list of contacts and their details for a specific set of conditions. A number of examples are given below:

1. A list of all the safety managers (and their telephone numbers) in the petrochemical industry whose offices are in Aberdeen where:

   Position = Safety Manager **and**
   Industry = Petrochemical **and**
   Postcode = AB2

2. A list of all technical editors of magazines, newspapers and journals in the construction industry (with their fax numbers) where:

   Position = Technical Editor **and**
   Industry = Construction **and**
   Category = Press

The same principle can be used for finding a particular company or person in a company, for example:

3. Find the telephone number for Mr Julian Goldsmith, who works for the Gofast Driving School, where:

   First name = Julian **and**
   Last name = Goldsmith **and**
   Company = Gofast Driving School

As well as searching for specific people or companies, you could also print out a complete list of contacts from your database. This can be useful when you are away from the office, providing a personalised telephone and address book of all your business contacts.

The disadvantage of the database is that it needs to be kept up to date on a regular basis. Business contacts are continually changing in companies – either moving offices, gaining promotion (or losing their jobs) and, with new telephone switchboard technology, changing their direct dial telephone numbers. Keeping a database up to date is therefore more time-consuming than you think. It is best done on a regular basis, which is all part of the process of being organised. Every time you make a new contact, type it in straight away and every so often, list the entire database and delete contacts that are no longer relevant. If the database grows too big with redundant entries, you will find that you get presented with useless information. *Rubbish in = rubbish out.*

Database software price range
£30 – £250

Sending regular mail-shots

One of the greatest benefits of keeping an up-to-date database of contacts is that it makes it much simpler and quicker to keep in written contact on a regular basis. For example, you may want to send regular press releases to a specific set of trade magazines. It is much better if you can personalise this process with a letter to a named individual, and, if appropriate, be able to use their first name – 'Dear Quentin', or whoever. It takes time to collect and update such information, but if you want to send out regular press releases that get noticed, it is well worth while.

In the same way, it can also be good public relations to keep both your existing and potential customers informed of your business progress, such as new contracts and orders, new products and services, change of address and so on. It is very easy when you are working on your own to get bogged down with everyday work and forget that you are losing contact with these customers. Remember that you don't have a salesman to do this for you. So keep the customers informed and never let them forget you.

Mail merging – the ability to type a letter once and allow the computer to automatically address and personalise it to your selected contacts – is achieved by using a word-processor in conjunction with a database. Very simply, you can select the contacts that you want to mail from your database, in the same way as preparing database lists, described earlier. You then need only type a letter once on the word-processor and by a little jiggery pokery it will automatically print this same letter to all the people on the list – personalised with the individual names and addresses. Within half-an-hour, you can have written just such a personalised letter to 200 people or more.

Addressing envelopes

Although some printers will allow printing on envelopes, the unevenness of the envelope can give rise to both poor print quality and potential envelope jams in the printer. The alternative is to use A4 sheets of sticky labels. You put the sheets, containing about 16 sticky labels, through the printer in the same way as ordinary paper and set the word-processor up for printing on the particular size labels. If you use a laser printer, it is important to use special laser printer labels, otherwise the heat generated by the printer will destroy the standard type and with none too good an effect on the printer itself.

Such sticky labels are particularly useful when performing a mail-shot to a large number of customers, as the same database of names and addresses can be used to generate the address labels as well as the personalised letters.

If you are making regular mail-shots to large numbers of people, it is worth considering an additional printer that is dedicated solely to the task of label printing.

7

Communicating with the outside world

One of the major drawbacks of operating a home-based business has been how to stay in touch with customers and contacts when you are out. The answerphone is the most well-known technology tool for this purpose, though it has taken many years for this machine to be accepted. Even now, many people are shy about leaving messages on answerphones and prejudices still exist about businesses which use them.

These attitudes are changing due largely to the adoption of direct-dialled numbers and voice messaging systems in large companies, which allow you to by-pass the company's operator and leave messages in an individual's electronic voice message-box (a grand name for a glorified answerphone). As this trend for leaving messages with machines develops, many people are coming round to the idea that it can have advantages – they know that their message will get through accurately and reliably.

This is all good news for the home-based business as it means that the acceptance of answerphones is developing. But that is not the end of the story – there are numerous other technology tools that help communication. Not only the fax – the ability to send copies of paper documents via the telephone line – but also a whole array of new things you can do with your telephone. For instance:

- *Diverting your calls* to another number (you may be working for the day somewhere else or you want calls diverted to your mobile phone). This can include both your telephone and fax
- *Three-way telephone conversations* with other people in different parts of the country (or world)
- *Call waiting:* answering an incoming call while you are already using the same telephone line
- *Itemised telephone bills:* a subject close to all our hearts

- *Mobile telephone:* allowing you to keep in touch while out of the office (you can also divert your office phone to a mobile phone).

If you really want to impress your customers with your speed of response, you can use a voice messaging service that will alert you with a small bleeper when someone has telephoned you and left a message, making sure that you can get back to them straight away. Many mobile telephones now include such a feature as standard.

The widely used fax machine has revolutionised the speed at which organisations can send documents to each other and it has almost become a business necessity, particularly when doing business abroad, with its associated long postal times.

What's more, you can connect your PC into the ordinary telephone network to provide many new possibilities, such as sending and receiving information prepared on your PC to other people, provided each PC has a device called a modem to connect it to the telephone line. The most popular way of doing this is via the Internet (or 'information superhighway') and this is described later on in this chapter. Some home-based businesses, such as consultancies, send their word-processed documents to their clients and team members in this way and designers increasingly use this facility for sending their desk-top published materials to the printers to speed up the production process.

In the same way, the ability to connect computers using telephone lines allows you to dial electronic databases of information. As an example, you can dial into a *Financial Times* database of information about companies – how big they are, their turnover, who their key directors are, their products and markets and so on. This can be useful for market research, enabling you to identify companies and people you wish to contact. Such 'live' databases of information are always up to date and when you have found what you want, it is possible to retrieve this information via the telephone line on to your own PC, enabling you to use it in word-processed documents.

This whole range of facilities is almost overwhelming. It is the start of an era where your office can be located almost anywhere and it means that you do not have to be cut off from the outside world when working from home.

Telephones

No longer are you restricted by British Telecom to rent their telephones – you can now choose from a wide variety of brands and buy them in high street shops. Generally speaking, the more you pay, the more features (and often gimmicks) you get, for example:

- *Hands-free:* a small loudspeaker allows the telephone to be used without having to put the receiver to your ear. This is useful while waiting for calls to be answered (you can get on with doing other things), though using the loudspeaker once the call has been answered does not do anything for speech clarity at the other end of the line!
- *Stored numbers:* regularly dialled telephone numbers can be stored in the telephone's memory and recalled by either pushing a button or entering a short code.
- *Last number redial:* a single button to press which redials the last number you called (useful if you keep getting an engaged tone).
- *Display incoming number:* when the telephone rings, the caller's telephone number will be displayed (though this does not work for all calls, for instance international calls, or where the caller has chosen to withold the display of their number).

Of more importance than the gimmicks is the type of telephone you should buy, being broadly divided into three categories: the older pulse-dialling telephones, the newer touch-tone phones and those touch-tone phones that include a Mercury button.

Pulse-dialling telephones are rarely sold these days and can mostly be recognised by the traditional dial. These types of phone should not be considered for your home office as they will not be able to take full advantage of the newly modernised digital telephone exchange services (described later).

Touch-tone telephones use push-buttons instead of a dial and will look like Figure 7.1, though beware, not all push-button telephones have a touch-tone facility. Check this carefully when you buy. These telephones provide quicker and more reliable calling and access to new services when used with the modernised telephone exchanges.

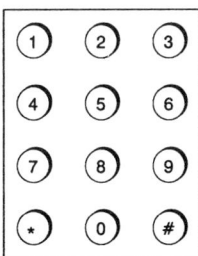

Figure 7.1 *Touch-tone telephone pad*

A Mercury telephone is a touch-tone phone which has a Mercury button, allowing you to use both BT and Mercury telephone lines with the same telephone. If you make many long-distance calls, it is a cost-effective proposition to buy one, though Mercury telephone lines can be used without necessarily buying one of these telephones (see page 90 for more details).

All touch-tone telephones are now widely available and, provided you have one of the standard BT sockets in your home-based office (a white box in which you plug the small white connector on the end of the telephone), it is simply a question of plug and phone. If you still have the old style telephone sockets (either the phone is wired into the socket or the connector is a rather chunky plug), you will need to get BT to change your socket to one of the small white box types.

Occasionally you will come across telephones and other equipment that plug into the phone socket (such as a fax or answerphone) which have not been BT approved (authorised equipment has a 'BT approved' sticker). Beware of this as it is a condition of using BT lines that you only connect equipment that has their approval.

There are many other options available when it comes to buying a telephone and this chapter describes some of them, such as:

- Combining it with an answerphone in a single machine
- Combining it with an answerphone and fax in a single machine
- A portable telephone that can be carried around the house (and garden) without any connecting lead (not to be confused with mobile telephones)
- A mobile (or cellular) phone that can be used almost anywhere in the UK
- A small switchboard that allows you to have several telephone lines and many extensions around the house, enabling you to switch different calls to different extensions.

Telephone price ranges
Touch-tone phone £15 – £90
Portable phone £60 – £110
Combined phone/answerphone £70 – £200
Combined phone/answerphone/fax £400 – £900
Mobile phone £50 – £400
Switchboard £450 upwards

Mobile phones

Although based in the home, you are likely to spend time out and about and a mobile phone (or cellular phone) can certainly help you in a number of ways, for instance:

- You can make calls wherever you are in the UK, as these phones do not use the traditional phone lines but transmit calls via the air waves, and therefore should not be confused with portable phones that are used purely in and around the home on the traditional BT lines.
- You can receive calls in the same way, as you are given a separate phone number from your office one.
- You can divert your normal office line to a mobile phone using the 'call diversion' facility, (described on page 127); it means that people calling your office number will automatically be transferred to your mobile phone – without realising it.
- A mobile phone can be installed in your car (and some will allow you to take it out of the car as well) to make use of time spent in traffic jams on our over-crowded roads.

The mobile phone companies will also provide a 'voice messaging' facility (sometimes at extra cost) that will allow you to divert your incoming mobile phone calls to a voice message-box if your phone cannot answer the call; for instance, if it is switched off, engaged or, as sometimes happens, the phone is in a poor reception area and the signal is not strong enough to be received. The messaging works in the same way as an ordinary answerphone – the caller is answered with your message and invited to leave their message. You can then dial in and pick up your messages as if you are using an answerphone.

It is possible to link this messaging service with a pager so that when a message is left, a small device that you carry around with you (sometimes it is included with your mobile phone) will bleep an audio signal that alerts you to the fact that someone has left a message. Paging is described in more detail on page 129.

Mobile phones have come a long way in recent years and are now much lighter than they used to be – they really are mobile! When buying one the major issues are how heavy it is and how long the batteries will last.

A word of warning on cost, though. The line rental and call charges are generally more expensive than for ordinary telephone lines, though with time, it is likely that they will become more comparable. What's more, you should be careful when signing contracts for a mobile line rental. 'Special deals' are commonplace, offering a cheap phone, if you sign up for a long period of line rental. Even if you don't make any calls, these deals will always cost you a lot more than the price of the phone and frequently have severe cost penalties if you try to cancel. So beware, *read the small print very carefully,* and work out exactly what it will all cost before you sign on the dotted line. Mobile phone services have proliferated recently and tariff structures can sometimes be confusing. It is usually best to anticipate the number of calls you are likely to make and when you will make them and then work out the most economic deal – taking into account the cost of the phone, the line rental and likely call charges.

Mobile phone price ranges
Phone cost £50 – £400
Line connection charge £10 – £70
Monthly line rental £12 – £30

Call charges
many different (and sometimes complex) tariffing structures ranging
from free off-peak local calls to 33p per minute for a national call

Additional costs for car phone
Installation £80 – £100
Car adaptor £200 – £400

What Mercury and other service providers have to offer

When British Telecom lost its monopoly on providing phone services in the UK, Mercury Communications became their competitor, or at least, up to a point. Mercury cannot offer an entirely separate phone service as their telephone lines are mostly long-distance as opposed to local ones. A Mercury long-distance line is therefore reached via your normal BT line and so you do not need a new line or telephone number.

When you make a Mercury call the long-distance part of the call will go via the Mercury lines and the local part via the BT lines. Mercury will send you a bill which covers both their charge and BT's, (you will not be charged by BT as well). The advantage of using the Mercury service is that their long-distance call charges are cheaper than BT's.

The Mercury service is therefore a cost bonus addition to your existing BT phone line and number. In order to use it, all you need do is pay a small annual subscription to Mercury and either:

- Dial a prefix of '132' before any long-distance or international call; or
- Buy a Mercury compatible phone; it has a special button which you press when you want to make a call using the Mercury lines (you pre-program the Mercury button with your Mercury account number); or
- If you are concerned that you may not remember to press the Mercury button or dial '132', Mercury provide a small box that sits between your telephone and wall socket, which does not require a Mercury telephone. This box will automatically 'decide' whether the call is local, long distance or international and route the call via a BT or Mercury line, whichever is appropriate (ie cheapest). However, the box will not allow extension phones around the house to have the same capability, unless they too are plugged directly into the box.

A Mercury facility makes no difference to your existing BT phone line and number – you use this as usual. But it is worth using the service for long-distance and international calls to give you the savings in call costs. They will be dependent upon the number of calls you make and what percentage are long distance. Mercury claim that you can save an average of 19 per cent on long-distance calls and 24 per cent on international calls. Because you have to fork out for joining Mercury and buy a compatible phone, it is probably only worth considering if your quarterly BT bill is in excess of £100 and if you are making many long-distance or international calls. Charges are changed from time to time (BT and Mercury are in competition after all), so you should contact Mercury for their latest rates and compare them with BT's to see if it is advantageous to install a Mercury facility. They provide simple tables showing cost comparisons between the two companies so you can easily identify the potential cost savings that you will make. Check for yourself by getting the calculator out!

Other features that Mercury offer are:

- Calls are charged for the exact time you spend on them and are not rounded up to the next unit (BT, however, are to start this shortly).
- You can arrange a special code to group calls into categories, say, separate ones for home and business use, and the itemised bill then

identifies these two separate groups; this is very useful when the VAT man and tax inspector visit!

Mercury charges
Annual fee £24
Mercury compatible phone £20 – £60

Mercury is not the only organisation that offers an alternative to BT. The emerging cable TV companies frequently offer similar low-cost telephone services and some even offer free local off-peak calls when both callers are connected via their own cable network.

Answerphones

The answerphone has not changed that much over the years, except that is now cheaper to buy. It is a simple device, requiring only a connection to the telephone line in conjunction with the telephone, using a small two-way adaptor. You can record a message that will be announced when you are out, asking the caller to leave their message. When you return, you can then play these messages back. You can also be sneaky; if you only want to talk to certain people, it is possible to leave the machine on while you are in and listen to the caller's message. If you want to talk, you can then pick up the telephone and the answerphone will switch itself off. This can backfire, of course, if the caller doesn't leave a message!

On the more sophisticated machines you will find extra features, for instance:

- A facility to allow you to call in to your own answerphone when you are away from the office and instead of leaving a message, to dial in a special code (known only to you) to play back any messages that have been received;
- A facility to use the machine as a dictation machine; it saves having to buy a separate one;
- An ability to record telephone conversations; this can be useful, but remember that the machine has by law to sound a small beep to the other party, alerting them to the fact that the conversation is being recorded.

Answerphone price range
£60 – £150

The message that you record, which is played to callers, can say a lot about you and your business. If you are nervous about leaving a message, it is likely that this will come over to potential customers, which will not give them a good impression. Try these tips:

- Listen to other people's messages recorded on their answerphones to get ideas on what to say and the way that you should speak.
- Practise recording the message a few times.
- Be original in what you record so that it will create an impression that will last.
- Make clear what information you would like the caller to leave.
- If you feel that you don't have the dulcet tones for the job, ask a friend to help you out.

An alternative to the answerphone is to use the voice messaging services that both BT and Mercury offer. It is a little more complex and expensive than an answerphone but has the advantage that once callers leave a message, you can be alerted with a small bleeping device. This has become commonplace with mobile phones, though not many people use it with their home-based telephones. To use such a service, all you have to do when you go out is redirect your office phone to your voice–message box telephone number using the BT call diversion facilities (more about this on page 127). Until you reverse this process, the voice–message box will act like an answerphone.

On phoning a potential client in a big corporation recently, a voice message on her direct dialled number announced 'Hi, it's Sonya – you know what to do'. Now Sonya may have been making false assumptions, but, as they say, 'It's not what you say, it's how you say it'. Such messages certainly reflect the greater acceptance of answerphones in business life.

Telex

Telex machines are becoming outdated now, particularly with the advent of fax machines. However, there are some industries and some parts of the world which still use them. They have one advantage over faxing – the sending and receiving of a telex can constitute a legal document, and industries such as the petroleum industry still find this useful. Sending a telex requires a separate telex machine which allows you to type text messages and send them to other telex machines, using a separate network of lines throughout the world, which are unconnected with the telephone line network.

If your work requires you to send and receive telexes, the other option, rather than buying a separate telex machine, is to subscribe to an on-line service, for instance, CompuServe (see page 133). This allows you to send and receive telexes in the same way as you send and receive electronic mail messages.

Fax

On a simple level, a fax can be thought of as a facility for sending post to people using a telephone line. All that is needed is for each party to have a fax machine, connected to their ordinary telephone line. It acts rather like a photocopier, allowing you to scan a document and the copy comes out on the other person's fax machine, instead of yours. In the same way, other people can send documents to you. It works like this:

- You place the pages of your document in the document feeder of your machine.
- You dial in the other person's fax number.
- Your fax machine calls the number you have dialled and the other person's machine will automatically answer the call, recognising that it is a fax machine that is calling.
- The pages are then automatically fed through your machine and almost instantaneously a copy appears at the other machine.
- When all the pages have been sent, both fax machines finish the call.

Faxing has become commonplace and many businesses have at least one machine. The great benefit is the speed of sending a document – it arrives almost instantaneously, rather than waiting for the post. In business terms, this can be invaluable – the more so when there is a postal strike.

Fax price range
Fax machines £150 – £1500
Fax calls charged at normal BT or Mercury rates

There are, however, a number of downsides of sending information by fax, which even people who use them regularly sometimes forget:

- The quality of the print is not the same as, say, printing on a laser printer; however, for ordinary type (of reasonable size) or handwritten materials, faxes are perfectly readable – it is only when people use small typefaces that they become difficult to read. The quality of what comes out the other end is not always the same as when it goes in!

- Many faxes use rolls of thermal paper, which over time, tend to fade, so always make photocopies if you have been sent valuable information via fax. To avoid this, fax machines are available which use ordinary A4 plain paper, though they are usually a little more expensive than the thermal paper type.
- Faxing information can be expensive, particularly if sending a long document. Remember, all the time the fax is scanning each page, you have an open phone line which is mounting up the telephone bill, particularly if it is peak-call time. It is often tempting to fax all your documents, but bear in mind that the post is a lot cheaper!
- It is sometimes tempting to send documents that have a legal status by fax (eg purchase orders, contracts), though it must be remembered that, strictly speaking, fax documents do not constitute a legal document, so it is important that you also send all such legal documents through the post.

Fax machines come in all shapes and sizes, with various features – some useful, some gimmicks. The important features to look out for are:

- *Document feeder.* Some fax machines will only take a small number of pages at one time, which means that, for a long document, you will have to stand over it and feed the pages in. This can be irritating so, if your budget permits, get one that will suit your likely requirements.
- *Grey scale.* Faxes work best when the document is purely black and white, though sometimes you may need to send information that contains shades of grey (eg a newspaper photograph), in which case you should consider a fax that has this capability.
- *Page cutter.* Most faxes use rolls of thermal paper so the faxes you receive will come out in a continuous roll. You can, however, get one that will automatically cut the paper into sheets or you could buy a plain paper type.
- *Telephone inclusion.* Many faxes come complete with a telephone, so you can use the same telephone line both for faxes and making and receiving calls. They will recognise an incoming fax as opposed to an ordinary telephone call (more about this below).
- *Answerphone inclusion.* Some faxes will also include an answerphone as well as a telephone (see below).

- *Stored numbers.* Fax machines usually allow you to store regularly dialled numbers and then either push a single button or type a short code to dial these numbers – it all helps to save time.
- *Photocopier.* Some faxes will allow you to use them as a photocopier. This facility can be useful if you are not going to be a 'heavy' photocopier user.
- *Broadcasting.* If you frequently need to send the same fax to many people, some machines will allow you to do this without having to scan the pages for each number you have dialled.

An alternative to fax machines is to buy a fax/modem for your PC, which allows you to send and receive faxes from your PC. You would typically use your word-processor to prepare a fax and, with the fax/modem connecting your PC to the telephone socket, instruct the PC to send it. Similarly, incoming faxes can be viewed on the screen or printed out. However, if you want to be able to send documents that have not been prepared on the PC, then you would need to connect a scanning machine to it. This is a more expensive and complex option than a dedicated fax machine and should only be considered once you are experienced with your PC, but it is handy when used with a portable PC, allowing you to send faxes when you are out of the office.

Telephone, answerphone and fax on one line

If money is really tight, you can operate a telephone, fax and answerphone on one telephone line. This saves on the costs of installing a dedicated fax line *and* the additional line rental. The best option is probably to buy a single machine that provides all these facilities in one. They work by recognising whether an incoming call is a person or a fax machine. An incoming call is first answered by the machine, which will recognise if a fax is calling. If it is, the fax process will commence; if not, the telephone will then ring and, if the answerphone is turned on, this will automatically operate.

Alternatively, you can buy a separate switch box that your telephone, answerphone and fax plug into, that will perform the same service.

Some of these devices cannot, however, recognise all fax machines and you should check this when buying. They are also not suitable for use with extension telephones in the home and should therefore only be used if you have a single telephone point. One further disadvantage is that some devices will play a computerised prerecorded message to the caller, while it is 'deciding' whether an incoming call is a fax or an ordinary call. These messages do nothing for the company image and you should check exactly how the device works before buying.

In view of the disadvantages of these devices, it is worth considering installing a separate fax line, particularly if you are likely to be a frequent user of a fax machine: remember, while the fax is operating, it is blocking the ordinary telephone line.

Combined fax, phone, answerphone price ranges
Combined phone/answerphone/fax £400 – £900
Phone/fax switch box £30 – £70

Doing more than you think with the telephone line

Some new BT services are now available, provided you have a touch-tone phone and live in an area of the country which has one of the modernised exchanges. They are called Star services and you have to pay a quarterly rental for them, in addition to the normal line rental. They are worth considering and are ideally suited to the small home-based business (you can find out more about them by calling BT sales).

Star services price range
£4 – £18 quarterly rental

You use the services by typing in various codes using the keypad. Some of the codes can be difficult to remember at first, but after a while you get used to them. The services include:

- *Call diversion.* This allows you to divert your telephone calls to another number (not just in the UK), by typing a special code and then the number that you want your calls to be diverted to. When a caller dials your number, it will instantly ring at the number you have provided and will even work in the same way for a fax line. It means that you can take your office anywhere; don't forget, though, that you pay for the diverted call from your office to its destination.
- *Three-way conversations.* If you need to talk in a group of three people, all of whom are on different telephone numbers, you can make one call (or it can be an incoming one) and then dial the other number to hold a joint conversation.
- *Call waiting.* This service allows you to interrupt a call to answer an incoming call on the same telephone line. It works as follows: if

you hear a small bleep in the middle of a call (the person you are speaking to cannot hear it) it means that someone else is calling; the new caller, instead of getting an engaged signal, hears a message asking them to hold on; you can then switch between the two calls, treating the phone as a small switchboard.

- *Out-going call barring.* This feature allows you to bar certain types of call, for instance, international ones. It can be useful if you are concerned that unauthorised use of your phone is taking place; the feature can be cancelled by typing in a special password code that only you know. It can also be used to bar the premium rate calls which have been known to cause excessive phone bills.
- *Charge advice.* If you want to know how much a particular call costs, you can type in a code before making the call. Once the call has finished, you will be told how much it costs (a computerised voice phones you back with the information). Alternatively, you can arrange to have all calls itemised and the information will appear on your bill.

BT also differentiates between residential and business lines. On the one hand you pay more for a business line (currently connection is approximately £30 more and line rental £10 more), though you do get quicker response if things go wrong, and your company details are inserted both in the business directory and *Yellow Pages*.

Using other people's phones without landing them with the bill

If you are out and about a lot and frequently need to make phone calls, there is an economical alternative to buying a mobile phone – using a charge card. This card allows you to make calls from any phone (such as your customers' or pay-phones) and have the cost of the call charged to your own phone bill. All you need to do is to find a touch-tone phone and dial a special number. You then key in your charge card number, a security code and the number you wish to dial. The cost of the directly dialled call is charged to your own account and costs no more than if you were phoning from your office. You can also do this from a non touch-tone phone, though you have to go through the operator – and you will be charged extra for this.

You should be careful about using these charge cards in companies which have modern switchboards that record all details of telephone calls, as they will also record the codes that you dial in – these contain your charge card number and your security code. You could then be liable if unauthorised use were made of the card.

Charge card prices (above normal call charge)
Direct dialling: none
Via the operator: 46 pence

Paging

If you have very demanding customers or colleagues who frequently need to contact you quickly and you can't afford a mobile phone, it is worth considering a radio paging system. You are given a special telephone number and a small device that you carry around with you – it either has a simple audio bleeper or a small display on which messages are displayed. They work in one of three ways:

- *Bleeper only.* Your caller will phone your special pager number (they do not need to do anything else) and this will automatically alert your bleeper by sending a radio signal. This presupposes that you know what to do when you receive the bleep; it may be to ring into your answerphone to pick up a message, or call a special customer who you have given your number to.
- *Telephone number display.* Your caller will dial your special pager number which will be answered by an operator, who will ask for a contact telephone number. The operator will then send a radio signal to your bleeper which will display the contact telephone number for you to ring. The caller can alternatively do the same thing without having to go via the operator, by using a touch-tone telephone to type the contact telephone number themselves.
- *Message display.* This works in the same way as the telephone number display, except that your caller can have a text message displayed on your device as well as a telephone number, though there is no automated alternative for this option – the caller must go via the operator.

Paging price range
'Bleeper' (monthly) £18 – £20
Telephone number display (monthly) £30 – £35
Message display (monthly) £43 – £46
Connection charges (one-off) £20 – £30

You can link a bleeper pager with a voice messaging service (described on page 93). If you have diverted your office or mobile telephone to your voice message-box, the caller is asked to leave a message (just as with an answerphone). Once they have left it, your bleeper will automatically be alerted to warn you that there is a message waiting.

Voice messaging price range
Registration fee £20 – £25
Monthly rental £10 – £12
Typical access charges:
...local 15p per minute
...national 20p per minute
...international £1 per minute
Pager link £2 – £3 per month

If you're working with other home-based offices

Some home-based businesses are more than just one person – maybe there are a number of you working from your own homes, dotted around the country. You may each be using your PC to work on a particular word-processed document and want to send it to each other to make modifications. One possible option is to post a floppy disc with the file on it, but this means waiting for the post to arrive. Alternatively, you could print the document and fax it – but the other person cannot alter the fax itself – they would have to scribble on changes and fax it back to you.

The ideal solution is to use the telephone lines to send the word-processed file itself. And this can be carried out simply. All you need to do is to buy a small device called a modem that will link your PC to the telephone line, together with communications software for the PC that will help to operate the modem (the two often come bundled together). See Figure 7.3.

Price ranges
Modem £100 – £600
Communications software £40 – £150
Call charges: as for normal BT and Mercury calls

My own business is advising large corporations to fully exploit technology, not just to improve their everyday productivity and efficiency, but to help them use it in new ways. For instance, the PC's ability to process sound and video (called multimedia computing) can provide novel sales and marketing aids (eg computerised interior design) and can make staff training more effective with interactive multimedia training programmes, such as for management and communications skills development.

I work with other home-based businesses, where we put teams together for individual projects, which reflects developing new-style small-business networking.

The major business requirements are three-fold. First, clients expect high quality documents – reports, letters, brochures and so on; second, speedy commmunication with clients and team members is essential for fast-paced projects, and lastly, administration time has to be kept to a minimum. It goes without saying that costs have to be kept low.

The office computer is a Gateway 2000 P5-90 Pentium PC and high quality documents are produced using Microsoft Word word-processing software with a Hewlett Packard laser printer and a Hewlett Packard Deskjet colour printer. Drawings, illustrations, overhead projection slides and slide shows are generated using Microsoft PowerPoint presentation graphics software. Both these software packages are used by many of my clients, allowing us to exchange information electronically and in the same format.

Sending information electronically to team members and clients (mostly word-processed files), is achieved using a modem connected to the PC – which allows connection to their electronic mail systems using Lotus CCMail Mobile. Faxes are sent and received using a Brother 1000P Plain Paper Fax which also acts as a photocopier and faxes can also be sent direct from the PC using a US Robotics fax/modem in conjunction with Delrina Winfax Pro software. A Pioneer scanner provides a scanning facility that allows, for example, the scanning of photographs for incorporation into word-processed documents.

The same US Robotics fax/modem is used to dial into a number of different on-line services, such as CompuServe and the Internet. Both of these provide a range of different features, such as electronic mail, access to worldwide databases of information, news services, electronic trading (e.g. purchase of airline tickets) and contact and discussions with people around the world who have similar interests to my own.

One of the most useful, though currently expensive, tools that I use with clients is desktop video-conferencing. The Intel ProShare system allows us to see and talk to each other using our desktop PCs connected to an ISDN telephone line. Furthermore, it is possible at the same time to work on the same document together, for instance, a word-processed document – where both PCs will display the same information.

In addition to the office PC, I have a Sanyo notebook computer, which also has a modem and a fax built in, allowing both word-processed files and and faxes to be sent and received, worldwide. Furthermore, when away from the office, I use the notebook PC and modem to dial the office PC and retrieve faxes that have been sent to it and print them on a Canon portable printer.

Administration time is kept to a minimum by using a basic accounts software package called Money Manager (my financial transactions are not complex). Records of clients and press are kept on a database (Microsoft Access) which is used in conjunction with the word-processor to carry out mail-shots.

BTs Star services are useful for diverting calls to my mobile phone (Mercury One-to-One), for three-way conversations and for answering incoming calls when already on the phone. A Mercury facility provides cheap long distance calls and itemised billing.

The answerphone enables messages to be retrieved by dialling the office number and typing a special code and a BT chargecard provides flexibility for using pay-phones and other peoples' office phones.

The costs broke down roughly as follows: Office computer £2,000; Laser printer £600; Scanner £950; Fax £450; fax/modem £170; Software £600; Video-conferencing £1,800; Answerphone £100; Notebook computer with fax/modem £1,500; portable phone £200.

Figure 7.2 *The author's own business*

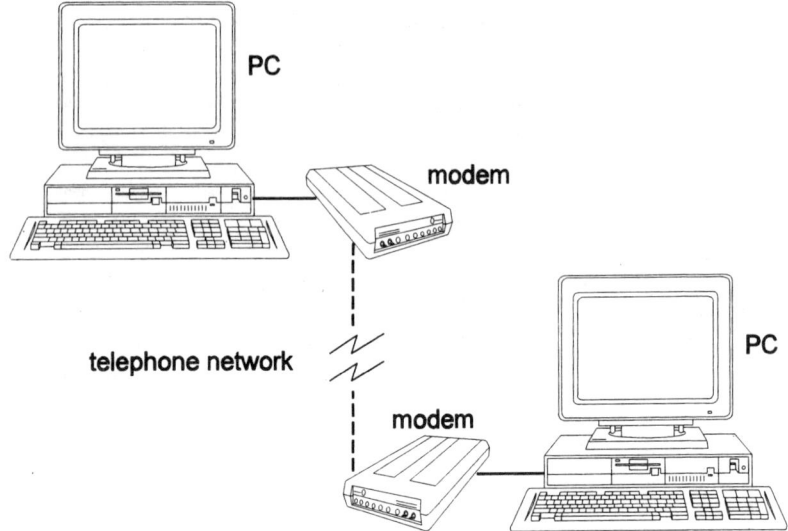

Figure 7.3 *Connecting two home office PCs together*

Modems can either be a small box that connects to the PC or they can be installed in the PC itself. A cable connects the modem to your telephone line. As with many other technology devices, there is a wide variety to choose from, though the key features to look out for are:

- *BT compatibility*. The modem must be approved for use with the BT phone network.
- *Speed*. The major difference between modems is how quickly they send data. The higher the speed, the more expensive they usually are, though you do then get cost savings on the reduced telephone call time; a minimum speed for most applications is 14,400bps though, if you can afford it, it is worth purchasing a 28,800bps or 33,600bps modem.
- *Hayes compatibility*. There is a universally accepted standard for modems called 'Hayes' and it makes sense to stick to this standard.
- *Intelligence*. Most modern modems will be fully automatic; for instance, they will save you having to dial the telephone number yourself (you previously store the number using the communications software) and they will also automatically adjust the speed at which they transmit data according to the speed of the modem at the other end of the line.

- Fax capability. Nowadays, it does not cost significantly more to buy a fax/modem – basically a modem that also has a facility that allows your PC to send and receive faxes (see page 126).

The communications software can vary tremendously from being able to perform simple transfer of your data files (eg word-processed documents) right up to allowing both PCs to work on the same document at the same time. It is probably best to use the software that comes bundled with the modem first and get used to it before you try anything too adventurous.

The method by which your communications software works will, in principle, be as follows:

- First you telephone your colleague and tell her to switch on her modem and plug it into the phone line; she should then start the communications software and set it to 'answer mode', ie for receiving a file.
- You then do the same except that you tell the communications software that you want to send, not receive, a file.
- You type in the phone number that you are sending the file to and instruct the software which file you want to send.
- It is then a matter of waiting for the file to be transferred to the other computer, after which you can both turn off your modems; your colleague now has your file to work on.

This method of transferring data files from one PC to another via the telephone network works not only for word-processed files but will work with any other type, for example, spreadsheet, graphics, and database files.

The information superhighway

A more flexible way of exchanging data files from one PC to another is to use the electronic mail and file transfer facilities offered by one of the many 'information superhighway' service providers, such as CompuServe. Instead of connecting two remote PCs together at the same time, all you need do, in order to send a file to your colleague, is to use your modem to send the file into CompuServe's computer – addressed to your colleague's mailbox address number. The file will remain stored in this mailbox until your colleague uses his PC and modem to dial into CompuServe's computer – at which point the file will be transferred automatically to his PC. Figure 7.4 illustrates how CompuServe's computer acts as a relay in sending the file. Using this method has a number of advantages compared with linking two PCs together directly:

● You can send a file at any time of the day or night – your colleague does not have to be around when you do this as the file can be retrieved from the mailbox at any time.

● You can send the same file to as many other people as you like, provided they have a mailbox address.

● What you send need not be a file – it can simply be a message, for instance, letting your colleagues know about a future meeting that you have arranged.

● The call charge will be relatively low, provided you are in or near a large city and, for many people, this will be at local call rates.

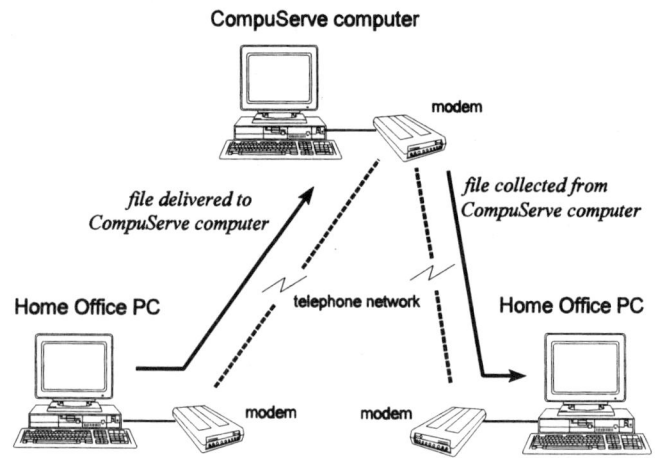

Figure 7.4 *Sending files via CompuServe*

Electronic mail and file transfer represent only a fraction of the facilities that service providers such as CompuServe offer. Other services include:

● *On-line information.* Using your PC and modem, you can dial into CompuServe's computer which holds a wealth of useful information. For instance, you can browse the European railway timetable and make bookings and reservations. Similarly, you can find out aircraft departures and arrivals information and make bookings and reservations. The AA (Automobile Association) provides information on CompuServe, including a 'Roadwatch' service which gives up-to-the-minute reports on traffic hold-ups, roadworks and weather conditions across the United Kingdom and a travel service that provides details of hotels, restaurants, travel routes, service stations, tourist information etc.

Business information is provided by Dun and Bradstreet and InfoCheck, giving up-to-date information on companies and company performance, and news is provided by the Press Association. It is also possible to get hold of up-to-the-minute stock prices, and scientific and technical information is provided by a large range of databases, such as *Chemical Abstracts*, where you can search the entire database for abstracts or articles by authors or subjects of interest.

While you are browsing through this information, your PC is 'on-line' to the CompuServe computer, and your next telephone bill will show a cost equivalent to making a normal telephone call. In addition to the charge for the telephone call, you may also be charged for the information services that you use. Prices vary depending upon the information that is being retrieved. For example, the AA Roadwatch service is free, while a search for a company profile could incur a charge of $50.

- *Electronic shopping.* CompuServe also features an 'Electronic Shopping Mall' that allows you to go on-line and browse and search catalogues of different products, such as books, computer products, CDs, gifts, office supplies. The catalogue typically provides details of the products and prices and, in some cases, pictures of the products. You can then place orders for products of interest and arrange for delivery and payment – usually via your credit card.
- *Forums or newsgroups.* These are one of most exciting aspects of information services such as CompuServe. Forums are accessed in a similar way to the information services described above – you dial into CompuServe's computer and select a particular forum, such as the 'Working from Home' forum. You can choose the 'library' section and browse through documents that relate to a wide range of subjects on working from home, for example, news and general information, how to get business, accounting and taxation tips, legal information, lists of associations and so on. Documents of interest can be selected and retrieved – the documents are automatically transferred from the CompuServe computer on to your own PC, where you can then read them using your word-processing software.

In addition to the library section, there is the 'discussions' section where a wide range of topics are discussed in relation to home working. These discussions are essentially a collection of electronic mail messages on a particular topic that are grouped together and which are continually being added to. For instance, you could start off a discussion by sending an electronic mail message, 'Do I need special insurance when working from home?' It is very likely that the next time you dial into the forum, you will have received replies to this question from a number of people and it may well start off a discussion – someone might give you the legal implications, others might recount experiences of not having an insurance claim met. These people may be anywhere in your local vicinity, in the UK, Europe, USA or many other places in the world. Forums are thus a 'meeting place' for people from all over the world who are interested in particular subject areas, enabling them to contribute towards discussions, seek advice and find useful information.

It is simple to subscribe to CompuServe; they will send you a floppy disc with software that will allow you to dial into their computer. Everyone pays a monthly subscription (approximately $8) which covers access to a wide range of basic information services and a certain amount of electronic mail messages. Access to forums costs more (typically $5 per hour) and other types of information services are charged under various tariffing structures.

The Internet

In addition to providing the information and communication services described above, CompuServe also allows you to access the Internet. The Internet grew out of the USA's defence research and education establishments and is essentially an extremely large collection of computers around the world that are linked together in a rather uncontrolled and unmanaged way. Its purpose was to allow research scientists to share information with each other but it has grown to such an extent that a large proportion of world-wide businesses have now 'joined' the Internet by connecting their computers to it. It has also attracted a large number of personal subscribers, who use their PCs to 'get on the Net'. This has spawned the growth of a variety of Internet Service Providers (ISPs) which, like CompuServe, will help you to gain access to the Internet. For an annual subscription of approximately £100–£150, they provide unlimited access to the Internet – allowing your computer to dial into their own computer system which is linked to the other computers on the Internet.

For the home-based business, the Internet offers many possibilities.

It allows you to send e-mails and files to any company or person connected to the Internet and you can participate in electronic discussions or 'news-group' – just like with CompuServe.

One of the most exciting parts of the Internet is using a piece of software called a 'Web browser' to browse Web pages on computer systems around the world. On a simple level, Web pages are just pages of information containing text and pictures. Many companies create their own Web pages in the form of an electronic brochure, promoting, for instance, their products and services. Each page has a unique address (composed of letters and numbers), which anyone in the world who has access to the Internet can type in to view the pages.

There are other ways that people can locate specific Web pages. The Internet has spawned a range of businesses that provide services to the Internet community. There are, for example, many directories or 'search engines' that you can use to track down specific Web pages. These directories allow you to type in words – it could be a company name or product – and you will instantly be provided with a list of Web pages that feature those words. In practice, you often get quite a large number of 'results' and, if so, you will have to do a bit of sifting to locate the exact ones you want.

You can then use one of the most interesting and important aspects of Web pages, called the 'hyper-link'. In your search results, the unique address of the Web page you are interested in is more than just the address. By clicking your mouse on it, your computer will 'jump' to that Web page and you will have found what you were looking for. The Web page may be on a totally different computer in a different part of the world – this will not be apparent to you and your telephone bill will only ever show the cost of the local telephone call to your Internet Service Provider. This hyper-linking is a key part of Web browsing and will help you to explore or 'surf' the Internet for information.

Some companies now incorporate 'news-group' or discussion forums with their Web pages. This is quite common with technology companies and as well as being able to read (Web) pages of product information you can view and participate in electronic discussions with the company and other users who are interested in the company's products. This is very useful if you want to ask technical questions about the products. For example, you could 'post' a question to the forum and you are likely to get replies from the company or other users – wherever they are in the world. This can be a much better way of getting help and support than trying to telephone the company's help line – where you often have to wait for some considerable time to get through to someone.

In practice, because there is so much information now available, you will have to do some 'detective work' to track down things that are of use to you, but if you are prepared to spend some time on the Internet, you may well find it a useful and enjoyable experience. In my own business, the Internet is extremely useful for finding out the latest product information from technology companies and for discussing different aspects of technologies with other users.

Some companies are now offering more than just information on their Web pages. They are providing a facility to allow you to order and pay for goods. Until fairly recently, you have needed to be careful about such services as there is potential for all types of fraud when sending details of your credit card via the Internet. It is possible for other users of the Internet to intercept any message that contains these details and then use them illegally. The more well known companies are using systems that provide greater protection and as these systems become more widely used, electronic shopping on the Internet is likely to grow very rapidly. As an example, a major food supermarket in west London now features an Internet electronic shop where you can browse and select groceries, place orders for them and have them delivered to your home.

As a small business, you can create your own Web pages to advertise your products and services. If you join an Internet service, part of the subscription package often includes a 'hosting' service – this means that the company will store your Web pages on their Internet computer, making them available to all other Internet users. You can create your own Web pages yourself – often using free software that you can download from the Internet – or the company will help you to do it for a fee. You will need to decide what you want to put in your Web pages and supply the appropriate text, pictures and graphics. If you really want to provide stunning Web pages, it is possible to include sound and video, but this requires a bit more specialist knowledge to do. One of the most important things to do in your Web page is to provide an easy means for people to contact you. This is easy to do – you can add a special button to your Web page that, when someone clicks on it, will automatically help them to send an e-mail to your Internet e-mail address. It is also important that you promote your Web site. On a simple level, you could include the Web address (and your e-mail address) on all your business literature – including business cards and letter-heading. If you really want to be clever, you should persuade other companies in your business area to make 'hyper-links' into your own Web pages, in exchange for doing the same for them.

As well as creating your own Web pages, there are all sorts of business possibilities that are being created on the Internet. As an example, the various Web directories or 'search engines' that allow you to use their computers to find information make their money out of the Internet from advertising revenue. This can be very useful for advertisers, because they can customise their advertising to suit the interests of the person searching. For instance, if someone searches for Web pages that contain references to cars, when the search results are presented, the adverts that are displayed can be limited to those that relate to cars. As you become familiar with the Internet, you will begin to realise the many possibilities for starting up a business that uses this new communications channel. The beauty of this is that you can do a lot of it from a home-based office.

CD-ROM

As well as accessing information 'on-line', such as via CompuServe, it is also possible to search large databases of information using CD-ROM (compact disc – read-only memory) technology. By connecting a CD-ROM drive to your PC (many new PCs now come with them ready-fitted), you will be able to insert published CD-ROMs, which look just like a compact audio disc, into the drive. CD-ROMs can contain a large amount of data – typically 650MBytes compared to a floppy disc's 1.44MBytes.

For instance, you may have purchased the JUSTIS CELEX CD-ROM that contains the full text of European Union laws and official information. You will be able to search and browse through the data without incurring any telephone or on-line charges. However, CD-ROMs will typically incur either a one-off cost or a subscription for frequent updates. In general, it is usually better (and more cost effective) to purchase a CD-ROM only if you want to search the database frequently and when it is not subject to frequent changes. If, however, you are likely to want infrequent access only, then it is probably better to use an on-line service.

ISDN

For most applications, using the ordinary telephone network works perfectly well. If, however, you begin to use information superhighway services extensively, it may be worth considering using a new service called ISDN 2 (Integrated Services Digital Network: 2-line). This is a separate network that has been specifically designed for transferring high volumes of computer data. You are provided with two telephone lines and, with a special ISDN phone, you can use the lines as two normal telephone lines. The main benefit is that the ISDN telephone also allows you to connect your PC to the two lines, enabling both of these to be used to transfer high volumes of computer data. This can be particularly useful when accessing services such as CompuServe and the Internet which are increasingly providing computer data in multimedia format, eg pictures, sound and video, and which can take a long time to transmit when using ordinary telephone lines.

The disadvantage of ISDN is that it costs more to install than a traditional phone line – also bearing in mind that two lines are being installed, though the national call costs are the same. Furthermore, as time goes on, modem manufacturers are doing increasingly clever things in the design of modems to speed up the transfer of information on ordinary telephone lines. Many industry experts maintain that there is not a huge advantage in having an ISDN line these days for applications such as accessing the Internet. It is therefore probably only worth installing ISDN if you want two new telephone lines and/or the speed of transferring computer data is critical to you.

Integrated Services Digital Network prices
Connection charge £300
Quarterly rental £84 (2 lines)
Equipment £300 – £2000
Local/national call costs – each line is the same as ordinary telephone costs
International call costs – a premium charge for different countries

Desktop video telephony

If you really want to have the full technology works on your PC, you should consider desktop video telephony. At a basic level, this is simply a video-phone that allows you to see and talk to another person using your PC. You can dial them up and, with the aid of a small camera on the top of each PC, your respective pictures will appear on both PCs.

The most well-known system is the Intel ProShare system that requires an ISDN 2 line. This allows you to use the video-telephony feature with owners of similar systems and with systems that conform to an audiovisual standard called H320. This includes the big video-

conferencing systems that are commonly to be found in large companies. ProShare uses both of the ISDN lines to connect two PCs together
and therefore the (local and national) call costs will be double that of
an ordinary telephone call.

Such desktop video-telephony systems provide a lot more features
than just the ability to see and talk to others. One of the most useful
features is the ability to 'application share'. This enables two different
people to see and talk to each other, while at the same time displaying
the identical information on their PC screens. For instance, if you and
your colleague are jointly developing a proposal (word-processed)
document, by initiating the application sharing feature, you will both
see the document and any changes that either of you make to it.

The picture quality of such systems has yet to reach that which we
expect from, for example, video cassette recorders; however, as technology progresses, the quality improves all the time.

Similar systems, that work over a single (normal) telephone line and
which use very high speed modems (eg 28,800bps), are becoming
available, though the picture quality is not as good as systems such as
the Intel ProShare, that work over ISDN lines. However, as with
modern technology, it is likely that video-conferencing using ordinary
telephone lines will rapidly improve in quality and come down to a price
that is affordable.

Desktop video-telephony prices are falling rapidly and, at the time
of going to press, the Intel system is priced at £1200.

8

Keeping finances in check

Whatever business you are in, you will inevitably be making many financial transactions – sales and purchasing. In the early days of your business the number of transactions will probably be low and there is always the temptation to concentrate your efforts on selling and marketing the business, rather than organising a system for bookkeeping and recording all your financial details. Many people say, 'I'll sort that out when it becomes a problem'. The trouble is, it becomes a problem usually just at the time when business picks up and you need to devote all your energies to doing the work you've just sold – and you can suddenly find yourself with a complete muddle.

The best advice is to put time aside for getting your bookkeeping in order when you are starting the business. It will pay its way down the line in minimising administration time. It is here that technology can play a useful role, with the use of accounts software, to operate on your PC.

The gains from using accounts software will not only be in reducing the time spent on administering your financial transactions, but also:

- If you are registered for VAT, preparation of your VAT returns is greatly simplified.
- You can save on accountants' fees by automating the donkey-work, leaving the accountants to do what they do best, ie preparing your year-end accounts to give you the most tax-favourable benefits.
- If you keep records up to date, you will always know what your exact financial position is – what the bank balance is, who you owe money to and what monies are outstanding.
- Sending invoices, statements, reminder notices is greatly simplified. This means you are likely to collect your cash quickly (lack of cash is one of the biggest factors in ruining a business).
- If correctly set up, accounts software enables you to categorise all your financial transactions. As your business develops this means

that you can separate out monies expended on different clients or jobs and overheads, enabling you to identify the profitability of individual jobs or clients.

All the above can be done manually and, if your business makes very few financial transactions, you may consider that it is easier to use a manual system, backed up with the services of an accountant. But you can never get away without doing your bookkeeping – recording all your sales and purchases in a sensible and organised way so that you keep your accountant's fees to a minimum and provide information for tax assessment. In practice, you will also be making more transactions than you think – basic office necessities such as stamps, office supplies, telephone bills and so on – all these need to be recorded so you can get tax relief on them.

The great thing about using accounts software is that it provides a discipline for you to record all these transactions. If you do these as you go along, you then have all the information recorded for your VAT returns, statements and reminder notices and for your accountant to finalise your accounts and to provide you with information as to how well the business is doing.

As with many computer applications, the very act of implementing accounts software will necessitate that you get to grips with basic accounting practices and (if you don't already know), ensure that you more fully understand the financial basis of your business. Someone once said that he wanted to learn about a subject so he wrote a book about it (it was very successful). The very act of having to write in detail about a subject made him learn it. It's much the same with accounts software: in order to use it sensibly, you learn how accounting works.

Having said this, business owners are often overawed by the mystique of accounting and leave it either to their accountant, bookkeeper or member of their staff, being afraid that they will not be able to understand it. An example of this is Sarah, who runs a small company from home, importing furniture from Europe and selling it throughout the UK. Having decided to buy accounts software, she wanted to leave the purchasing and operating of it to her bookkeeper. However, she was advised to take control herself, despite the demands of a busy work schedule. Her reluctance to do this stemmed from a fear of not understanding bookkeeping and accounting practices, and she was afraid of letting her bookkeeper know this.

Specifying needs for accounts software requires that you know exactly the financial nature of your business and how it operates – you only have to miss one special feature that your particular business needs and the accounts package that you have just bought may turn out to be totally unsuitable. For instance, Sarah's business needs a multi-currency facility (she is importing furniture from Europe) and not all accounts packages have this feature – a small detail but it could render it useless. Furthermore, if Sarah had not taken control herself and left the choosing and operating of the accounts software to her bookkeeper and computer supplier, she would be at their mercy when they went on holiday or were no longer available – how would she manage then? It's also important to consider the possibility of fraud – if someone else is in total control of a computerised accounting system, it does give potential for them to exploit this.

Sarah was eventually persuaded to spend some time in researching what accounts software she needed and, once she started, she really got into it. She began to build up her confidence in dealing with the suppliers and in understanding much more about the financial side of her business. She is now glad that she didn't side-step the issue.

What accounts software will do for you

Sarah's business described above involves many transactions, as it was about buying a whole range of different products from Europe and selling them to a great number of customers, so she needed a fairly up-market accounts software package, with a number of different features including sales, purchase and nominal ledger, invoicing, invoice processing, report production and so on. Other businesses do not need such sophistication, for example small consultancies, where there are usually only a few clients. In this case invoices and statements can be prepared on the word-processor, using standard forms or templates. Similarly, such consultancies are unlikely to have a need for purchase order processing, stock control or payroll facilities, in which case the requirements for sophisticated accounts software are limited and a simple accounts package can be used.

First of all, a word of warning. Always go for an off-the-shelf accounts package. Do not, under any circumstances, let any technical friend of yours persuade you that they can develop a cheap software program for recording all your finances. It will be anything but cheap. As an example, a small home-based company got into a problem with their accounts software. It turned out that three years ago a technical friend of theirs had offered to 'help' them. First of all, he sold them a second-hand computer that was not a PC – it was a non-standard computer that was no longer being sold. Second, instead of providing an off-the-shelf accounts package, he said he would design one for them, using a database program as the 'core' of the package. Now this is perfectly feasible, but totally impractical. Accounts software packages take years of design time and there is no way that an individual programmer is going to be able to produce a similar result. The inevitable happened. First, the hardware, being non-standard and obsolete, became expensive to maintain – it was even difficult to find any company who would maintain it. Second, the accounts software was never finished properly and the technical 'friend' got bored with it and refused to finish it. The upshot was that the business acquired highly expensive hardware to maintain and an accounts package that only half worked. Furthermore, there were no manuals, so it was very difficult for the bookkeeper to use and it was virtually impossible for someone else to finish the software development – it would have required months of expert programming – an unrealistic proposition. The only practical solution was to start again with off-the-shelf accounts software and a standard PC.

Accounts software comes in all shapes and sizes to meet these diverse needs and prices range from £50 to £8000. The difference between them all is mostly down to the number of features, the size of company transactions they can process, the flexibility they have in adapting to different businesses, and the support you get – not only in advice on setting them up and running them but also relating to the comprehensiveness of the manuals and instructions.

In the early days of accounts software for the PC, the available packages were not always very effective – they were difficult to adapt for different businesses and did not come with readable and comprehensive manuals. They have come a long way since and there are now some very useful and powerful packages around. Most of them include such design features as:

- *Growth.* If you start off with very simple bookkeeping software and, as your business develops, your needs require sophisticated accounting, the software packages often allow you to do this without starting again – you can carry on with your existing accounts data.
- *Modular design.* In order to adapt to different businesses they will be designed in a modular fashion, eg sales ledger, purchase ledger, nominal ledger, payroll, stock control. This means that you do not need to buy all modules at once; you can learn to use the basic ones

first and then buy more as your knowledge and business grow; they become simple add-ons.

- *Tailoring.* Accounts packages allow varying levels of tailoring to suit a particular business, from simple setting of accounts codes and account classification right through to including a facility to enable development of specific applications.
- *Support material.* A variety of instruction books from simple 'getting started' to reference manuals, telephone 'hot-line' support and computer-based training material.
- *Report generation.* One of the most useful areas of accounts software is the report generator, where you can access information about your accounts in a whole variety of ways; this will, of course, depend upon how well you have classified your accounts, and can give such useful information as lists of outstanding creditors over three months, bank statements etc.

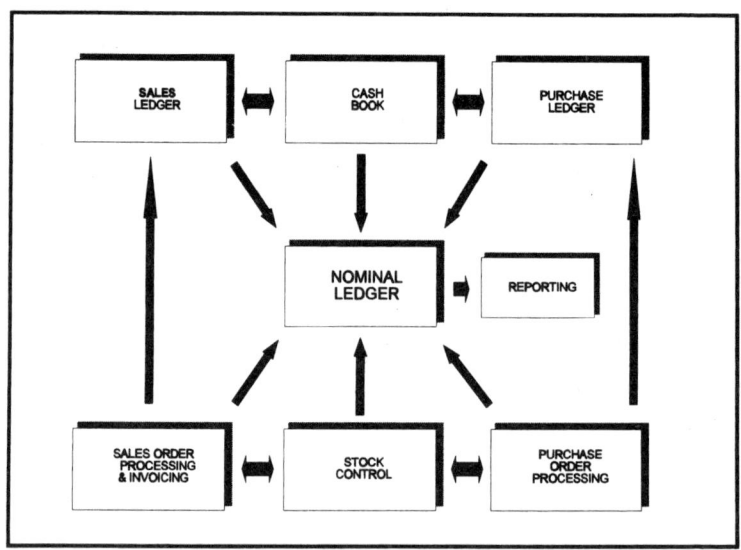

Figure 8.1 *Modular structure of accounts software*

Figure 8.1 illustrates how the basic functions of a typical accounts software are designed in a modular approach. The nominal ledger is core to all the various peripheral modules, such as sales and purchase ledgers, and it integrates all the transactions carried out in these modules. The modules are linked so that a transaction in one will also automatically be recorded in the others. For instance, a sales recorded in the sales order processing module will automatically update the stock control ledger, if relevant.

It is often possible to buy just the nominal ledger at first (to help keep costs down) and then buy the others as and when you need them. The peripheral modules make the task of using the nominal ledger simpler and quicker, though if your business does not require you to process many transactions in a particular module you may never need to buy it. For instance, if you make very few purchases for the business, it is probably not worth ever buying a purchase module.

The *nominal ledger*, as well as integrating all the various peripheral modules, will provide other features, such as trial balance, profit and loss, budget control and storage of historical data. There is usually a *report generator* that links to the nominal ledger, which enables you to extract information from your accounts and to tailor reports to suit the particular information that you regularly need. Information such as unpaid invoices, overall VAT analysis, monthly accounts, sales reports listed in various ways (eg by turnover or balance), list of customers by balance owing, list of overdue invoices and so on.

The *sales ledger* processes all aspects of sales accounting. You can define different VAT codes, create individual customer accounts (with names and addresses recorded) and produce individual account statements, eg aged debtors analysis, year-to-date turnover. Other features include part payments, prepayments, individual customer credit control, statement production and so on. The *sales order processing* module is a further addition to the sales module, which is particularly important for use with the stock control facility. It will automatically update records in the stock control module when a sale is processed and provides a number of other features such as automatic invoicing, order acknowledgement forms, despatch notes, reallocation of available stock, order status, despatch recording and so on.

The *purchase ledger* may not be necessary for a large number of home-based businesses unless there is a large number of purchase transactions from different suppliers. This module allows you to define individual supplier accounts, with names and addresses. You can produce individual account statements, such as aged creditor analysis, year-to-date turnover, VAT analysis, part and pre-payments and list of creditor balances. The *purchase order processing* module is essentially a sister package to the sales order processing module.

The *stock control* module will only be necessary if your business involves keeping stock items. It will record all information on individual items and their movement. Reports can be produced which also detail stock valuation, profit, and reorder reports.

The *cash book* keeps details of bank accounts, credit cards and cash, recording all payments, receipts, standing orders and direct debits. It will post these to the relevant accounts, eg individual customer or supplier accounts and provide a facility to help you reconcile your statements – allowing you to check your bank statements.

In addition to the basic modules described, the more sophisticated accounts software packages are likely to offer other modules, such as job costing and payroll.

Job costing will be useful if you are running a business where you undertake individual jobs that involve a large number of financial transactions and you want to be able to record and analyse the jobs in detail. For instance, if your company business involves putting teams of people together to undertake work for different clients, where the fees are time-based, it will allow you to record hours worked against the individual jobs, and assign all costs in the same way. It will link into the invoicing system in order to automatically generate itemised invoices. A facility is usually included to help you to budget these jobs and compare the 'actuals' with the budget – important information when you come to budget the next job as you can tell how good your estimating was!

Payroll is unlikely to be necessary for most home-based businesses as it is only worthwhile if you have a largish number of people on the payroll. It simplifies the calculation of wages, providing pay-slips with the appropriate deductions for National Insurance and PAYE and takes into account P35, P11, P14/P60, holiday pay and pensions.

Sorting out what you need

Buying accounts software is not as straightforward as say, buying a word-processing package. To a large extent, word-processors, in their basic form are much of a muchness: unless you have particular specialist needs, eg a multilingual capability, you cannot go far wrong with any of the major software packages. Though people often have strong views on individual word-processing packages, this often relates to their having learnt it in some detail and knowing its quirks.

It is not the same with accounts packages. It is important that you buy the appropriate package for your particular business. There are a large number of packages available which are geared to a wide range of businesses. In 90 per cent of cases, it is possible to buy a package that can be easily tailored to your business, particularly for small ones, where

Bert has a very profitable business in the motor trade – selling low-cost accessories to garages and work-shops. Bert started the business by selling key-tags, a small key-ring with a plastic label, on which details of a car can be written – owner, make, colour and registration number. They come in a box of 100, complete with marker pen, key-rings and labels. They are very handy for garages and work-shops who are servicing numerous cars everyday: it helps them to keep track of keys as cars come in and out. Bert has now expanded the business with other accessories, including security boxes to house the keys.

Bert buys the individual components (key-rings, labels, pens and box), assembles them and sells them on as a kit. He now has a flourishing business with a large customer base, now 'ripe' for marketing other products.

The kit is low-cost (£29) so the profit comes from bulk selling. As business started booming, Bert found that the paperwork was beginning to overwhelm him and he needed two clerical assistants to cope. He also found that his accountant's bill was mounting. At this stage he had the foresight to start computerising!

Bert had not used computers before and was slightly apprehensive about them. However, he overcame this and, from day one, decided to 'take control' himself. He approached a local supplier and worked with them to specify what he needed. Finally, he bought a powerful PC and two printers – a dot matrix and a laser – together with an accounts package and word-processor. The supplier installed the system, set it up and trained Bert to operate it.

The accounts package included sales, sales order processing, purchase, purchase order processing, stock control and nominal ledgers plus cash book. Bert didn't learn the system overnight – he continued to use the manual system as the primary records until he was totally familiar with the computer. His business continues to grow and he now manages all the accounts with the computer, with the help of one clerical assistant. With his present level of business, he now reckons that he would need three clerical assistants if he didn't have the computer (saving about £25,000 a year on their salaries and additional accountant's fees).

He is pragmatic about the computer and continues to keep all print-outs of data as a back-up. He also does regular daily, weekly and monthly data back-ups on to a magnetic tape back-up device that connects to the computer. This saved his bacon once when a power surge, caused by a faulty electricity supply, corrupted the hard disc of the computer – erasing much of the data.

All invoices, statements, remittance advices, order acknowledgements, purchase orders are generated via the accounts package and printed on to pre-printed forms which have carbon copy sheets. When existing customers phone in for another order he can immediately look up their details and check whether they have paid up to date and have not exceeded their credit limit.

He also uses the system to print aged creditor reports and send statements if necessary. He has all the customers' names and addresses stored, from which he can prepare mailing labels to market new products.

He has since updated his PC with a faster model and purchased a separate PC for his clerical assistant. In the near future, he is planning to connect the PCs together in a network, in order that they can share the same accounts and word-processed data.

The hardware comprises two Dell Pentium PCs (1GByte hard disc), an Epson wide-carriage dot-matrix printer and a Hewlett Packard laser printer. The accounts software is Pegasus Senior with the modules described above. The total price came to £5,000.

Figure 8.2 *Bert's motor trade business*

financial transactions are relatively simple. Also, if your business is just starting up, it is easier still – you will not have an historical method of organising and processing your accounts and you can develop a system around an accounts package. Here are a few tips to follow:

- The 'rules' in Chapter 5 are especially important when buying accounts software. Make sure you prepare a very detailed list of your requirements and ask your supplier to demonstrate the package in depth, showing applications that are as close as possible to your own business (sometimes you can get demonstration copies to try out on your own machine).
- Ask to see the manuals for the software and check whether you can understand them.
- Find out whether there is a computer-based training package to go with the product and try it out.
- Ask the supplier what support they will give, for example, on-site trouble-shooting visits, training and telephone hot-line; check how much it will all cost first.
- Check with your accountants what package they use; it might make great sense to use the same one.

The only exception to the above rules is if you want to buy one of the very cheap and basic accounts packages, where the cost is relatively small and it is almost worth just ordering it direct, eg a package called Money Manager – cost £50. Money Manager is a bookkeeping package, that allows you to assign simple account codes (clients, bank accounts, credit cards etc) and codes for individual clients or suppliers. It does not have the ability to assign individual clients' names and addresses, but does provide very detailed information if you set it up carefully, for instance VAT calculation, creditors/debtors lists. You can buy an 'add-on' to go with it called Final Accounts (cost £50) which provides more comprehensive information including profit and loss, balance sheet etc.

Another advantage of buying such a cheap package is that in getting to grips with it, you will learn a lot about accounting practice and, even if in time your business outgrows the package, you will have a much clearer idea about your future needs, without having gone to great expenditure. The downside is that there is no upgrade path for such a package so you would have to start again.

Now you've bought the package

Organisation is more important when using accounts software than with any other. Take note of the following rules:

● Frequent backing up of your data is crucial – not only daily, but also weekly and monthly (it is possible that your data gets corrupted and you don't notice until a couple of weeks have elapsed).

● Always assume the worst can happen with your accounts data, ie you could even lose all your back-ups, and produce regular print-outs of all your transactions.

● Always master the package yourself before letting others input data.

Making financial predictions using spreadsheet software

At some stage in your home-based business you may well need to borrow money from the bank, either to help get it going or to develop it. You may, for instance, need to finance some capital expenditure such as a fax machine or a PC. Alternatively, your need may be to help cash flow for an order (this is often a problem for the small business where suppliers are more likely to demand payment sooner than your customers are willing to pay). Bear in mind that it is usually easier to persuade the bank to lend you money to finance a confirmed order than to invest in your start-up idea. In many ways, this is not a bad thing as it is probably better to avoid borrowing money until you have a trading record: banks have a funny habit of 'pulling the plug' at any moment if they get twitchy about your business.

Having said that, there may well be times when you need to borrow money. At this stage you will need to convince the bank manager that your idea is sound and there is minimal risk. It is no good just having a conversation – the banks will inevitably ask for some financial projections so that they can assess the viability of a loan. They will want to know what income you will receive, what payments you will need to make and the timings of these various transactions, together with the probability factors. No one can guarantee anything in business – do not even attempt to convince the bank that you are 100 per cent certain! They will also want to work out whether you have clearly thought through all the issues and are capable of running a business.

You will probably be asked for a profit and loss prediction and a cash flow forecast for your business. Together, these will itemise all your outgoings and income in some detail and will show the timings, so that it is possible to estimate the amount of overdraft or loan that is required. It is usually a good idea to break down your outgoings into fixed overheads (usually payments that are necessary irrespective of what orders you have, such as telephone bills, subscriptions, office supplies) and cost of sales (payments that relate to a particular job you are doing).

Notwithstanding the banks' needs, this exercise is extremely good practice in any case. The reason is that it makes you consider how you are going to make money. You will have to think out all the details such as what your outgoings are going to be – telephone bills, stationery, purchases associated with your work, when you will get paid, and so on. It's quite surprising how, when you go through this exercise, it can raise issues that you had not considered – and it is far better to do this up-front, rather than getting into a mess down the line. Now, this doesn't mean that you are not going to take risks with your business – you wouldn't, after all, be starting one if you are not a risk taker – but at least it will give you a far better idea of what the risks are and identify issues that you can control and those you cannot.

Profit & Loss	Jan	Feb	Mar	Apr....	Total
Sales					
Product A	500	1,000	1,200	....	2,700
Product B	200	400	300	....	900
TOTAL SALES	**700**	**1,400**	**1,500**	**....**	**3,600**
Cost of sales					
Product A	150	300	360	....	810
Product B	10	20	15	....	45
TOTAL COST OF SALES	**160**	**320**	**375**	**....**	**855**
Overheads					
Telephone	0	0	400	....	400
Office supplies	25	35	90	....	150
Equipment maintenance	0	0	150	....	150
Legal fees	0	900	0	....	900
Accountant fees	0	0	400	....	400
Travel	90	56	67	....	213
Hire purchase	97	97	97	....	291
Postage	23	12	15	....	50
TOTAL OVERHEADS	**235**	**1,100**	**1,219**	**....**	**2,554**
Operating profit	**305**	**-20**	**-94**	**....**	**191**

Table 8.1 *Profit and loss prediction*

Table 8.1 illustrates a simple example of a profit and loss prediction for a business which sells two products, showing:

- the invoiced sales from January to March and giving the totals
- the cost of sales (this could be the cost of components)
- the fixed overheads – telephone, office supplies etc.

At the bottom is the calculated operating profit, which is calculated by subtracting the cost of sales and overheads from the sales.

Cash flow	Jan	Feb	Mar	Apr....	Total
Sales					
Product A	0	500	1,000	....	1,500
Product B	0	200	400	....	600
TOTAL SALES	**0**	**700**	**1,400**	**0**	**2,100**
Cost of sales					
Product A	150	300	360	....	810
Product B	10	20	15	....	45
TOTAL COST OF SALES	**160**	**320**	**375**	**....**	**855**
Overheads					
Telephone	0	0	400	....	400
Office supplies	25	35	90	....	150
Equipment maintenance	0	0	150	....	150
Legal fees	0	0	900	....	900
Accountant fees	0	0	400	....	400
Travel	90	56	67	....	213
Hire purchase	97	97	97	....	291
Postage	23	12	15	....	50
TOTAL OVERHEADS	**235**	**200**	**2,119**	**....**	**2,554**
Operating profit	**-395**	**180**	**-1,094**	**....**	

Table 8.2 *Cash-flow prediction*

Table 8.2 is similar but uses the same figures to predict the cash-flow – when monies are paid and received, rather than invoice dates. As you can see, the actual receipt of monies comes one month after the month of invoicing, though the cost of sales has to be paid straight away. Similarly, overheads are mostly paid immediately, though the legal fees (£900) in the month of February are shown as paid one month after invoicing.

Though the profit and loss prediction shows a minimum negative balance of £94 in March, in practice the cash flow prediction shows that an overdraft facility of £1094 would be needed in March in order to finance the work.

This exercise can, of course, be done with a calculator and, if your business is as simple as the one illustrated, this may be the best method. However, most businesses are more complex, in which case the calculator might need to go into overtime mode. Also, you might need to do the same calculations for a series of 'what-if' scenarios. For instance 'What if I sell less of product A in March – what effect will that have on the required overdraft?' or 'What if I don't get paid until two months after invoicing?'

This is where technology can help, using software called a spreadsheet. A spreadsheet can be regarded as the numerical equivalent of a word-processor. It allows you to create tables just as in Table 8.1, but instead of having to do all the calculations manually, you can type in formulas which will automatically perform the calculations for you. This means that when you want to find the answers for your what-if questions quickly, all you need do is type in new input data, for example, new sales figures for January – and the spreadsheet will straight away retotal them and readjust the results throughout the spreadsheet, right down to giving the new overdraft requirements.

The spreadsheet is based on a grid of cells, rather like a chess board. In any cell you can type either words, numbers or a formula. Table 8.3 illustrates such a grid, where any cell has a unique identifier, composed of a letter and number, based on the horizontal and vertical letters and numbers shown. Using the example of Table 8.3, the top left-hand cell will be identified as cell **a1** – it has the words **Profit & Loss** written in the cell, whereas cell **b5** has a number written in it (150). Cell **b7** could also be a number, but here is where the spreadsheet is really useful – instead it has a simple formula written in **b5 + b6** (the sum of cells **b5** and **b6**; 150 + 10 = 160).

In the same way, cell **b17** also has a formula **b4 - b7 - b16** (subtract cells **b7** and **b16** from **b4**; 700 - 160 - 235 = 305).

	a	b	c	d	e	f
1	Profit & Loss	Jan	Feb	Mar	Apr....	Total
2	Sales Product A	500	1,000	1,200	....	2,700
3	Product B	200	400	300	....	900
4	TOTAL SALES	700				3,600
5	Cost of sales Product A	150				810
6	Product B	10				45
7	TOTAL COST OF SALES	160				855
8	Overheads Telephone	0				400
9	Office supplies	25				150
10	Equipment maintenance	0	0	150	....	150
11	Legal fees	0	900	0	....	900
12	Accountant fees	0	0	400	....	400
13	Travel	90				213
14	Hire purchase	97				291
15	Postage	23				50
16	TOTAL OVERHEADS	235				2,554
17	Operating profit	305				191

Callouts in the table:

b5 + b6
(add cells b5 and b6)
150 + 10 = 160

b10 + c10 + d10 + e10
(add cells b10 ....e10)
0 + 0 + 150 = 150

b4 - b7 - b16
(subtract cells b7 and and b16 from cell b4)
700 - 160 - 235 = 305

Table 8.3 *Using a spreadsheet to do the calculations for you*

Now, if you go back and change cell b2 (the sales figure for product A) from 500 to 800, instantly, the spreadsheet will display a new set of figures (total sales in January will rise to 1000 and the operating profit for that month will rise to 605).

This is a very simple example and as you develop knowledge of the spreadsheet you can use quite complex formulas. In this way it's the same as a word-processor – you will develop increasingly sophisticated applications as you get to know all the features. For instance, Tables 8.1 and 8.2 showed a profit and loss and cash-flow prediction. You could include formulas which will specify the various payments timings – say, one month for your creditors and the same month for cost of sales payments. When you feed in your sales data, the spreadsheet will then automatically provide a cash-flow forecast.

Presenting your bank manager with a number of print-outs of your profit and loss and cash-flow calculations will impress her no end. It will also make you more confident in negotiating a loan or overdraft facility as you will have thought out every detail carefully. But do remember that you need to convince yourself first before trying to convince anyone else.

One of the other benefits of preparing your business predictions in this kind of detail is that you can include room for the 'actual' figures in your spreadsheet, ie the actual figures relating to monies paid out and received. This is very useful as you can check and monitor how good your calculations were; this means that when you are doing the next lot, your estimating process will learn from your earlier efforts.

Spreadsheet software usually includes a graphics facility that will allow you to present the information in graphical as well as tabular form – pie charts, bar charts, etc. This can also be very effective when you want to present information in a concise and easily readable way. But there are some reservations: financial graphs are sometimes used to mislead. For instance, it is common to find the labelling of the axes of a graph illegible or even non-existent, so that the graph will give a misleading impression. We have all seen graphs of rising sales of a company, only to find that when looking at the axes, it only takes account of the most favourable time period when sales were rising, but didn't show the falls as well.

One of the other advantages of preparing a detailed profit and loss and cash-flow forecast is that you will be communicating with the bank manager in 'their language'. I mean by this her *written* language. All financial people have a more or less standard way of looking at a business – through profit and loss, cash-flow forecasts and balance sheets. They are used to these methods of examining a business and, if you want to communicate with them effectively, you should use *their language*.

A technical director of a company was trying to convince the company accountant of the reasons why a particular product would not be a profitable one to sell. He tried talking and writing a report about it, but could not get the point across. Weeks later, he took advice and prepared a profit and loss forecast using a spreadsheet, showing how unprofitable the idea was (the cost of sales was going to be high and the overheads needed to be increased in order to sell the product). Within two minutes, the accountant understood the full implications – because the technical director was talking 'accountant's language'.

Other uses of a spreadsheet

The somewhat simplistic example of what a spreadsheet can do for you underlies the potential to which such software is capable. As you become familiar with it, there will probably be many applications you can use it for. As an example, Derek runs a business from home where he takes on contracts to design and build recording studios around the world. His company has been going for many years and is a good example of how even a company that undertakes large and complex contracts can still operate from a home base. Instead of having a permanent overhead of people, he puts together teams to carry out each project, doing the design work from London and then flying out the construction team to the country he is working in – only for the period of the contract.

Derek uses spreadsheet software for a number of applications, which start off with the acoustic design of the studio. He has to carry out a whole series of technical calculations to estimate what types of material are needed for the walls, ceiling and floors (eg the number of acoustic tiles). He also needs to calculate the noise levels from air conditioning equipment (to check whether it will be low enough not to interfere with sound recordings) and to calculate the noise penetration between studio and control room and to outside. Spreadsheets are ideal for this, as all the technical formulas can be fed in and, for each job, all he needs do is input the specific information related to that job. For instance, the area of walls and ceilings, the sound power level of air conditioning plant, the noise insulation of walls, and so on. Having this information stored permanently then makes the what-if scenarios simple to carry out: 'What if the architect wants to use a different type of glass for the windows – what effect will it have on the external noise level?'

He also uses the spreadsheet for pricing his jobs. He inputs all the price data on materials, sub-contract work, travel, accommodation, payments to the crew he hires (based on number of days worked), his own fees and so on, and the spreadsheet totals this all up. He can then use this model to calculate price variations if the client requires extra work, or if things don't go as well as he thought. Once he finishes the job, he also types in the actual figures – the total itemised prices, in order to check whether he got his calculations right in the first place. This provides him with useful information when he comes to his next quote – it tells him how good his estimates were and how profitable the job was.

This is just one example of how a spreadsheet can be put to very good use in a business, allowing the technical calculation time and job estimating time to be greatly reduced and carried out with a considerable degree of accuracy. No doubt your own business will be quite different from this, but the spreadsheet can be tailored very easily to your own requirements.

Do remember, though, that the predictions you make are only as good as the formulas and details that you use. There can be a tendency for people to take on trust information that comes from a spreadsheet just because it goes into a lot of detail and it looks good on paper. Though this is the intention – using it to convince people – don't make the mistake of falling for your own propaganda!

9

Polished presentation material

Companies, in particular the large ones, spend considerable sums of money ensuring that they present the right image to outsiders, in the form of full colour brochures, annual reports, TV, radio and press adverts, company videos etc. This also includes less direct ways of conveying the desired image – stylish office entrances, expensive office furniture, luxury cars for executives (sometimes cynically referred to as 'props'). The overall aim is to present a consistent and well-thought-out image to customers, press, suppliers and staff.

The small home-based business does not have the budget to compete with this type of expenditure; and nor should you even attempt to. However, with the aid of technology, some prudent expenditure and good design, it is possible to produce high-quality written materials which have a consistent and polished look to them, without the need for using expensive typesetting and printing companies. You can use the PC to produce your own letter-headings, with-compliments slips, business cards, proposals, reports (that include diagrams, schematics and drawings), overhead projection slides and colour slides. These materials will not match the quality of the full colour corporate brochure, but it is surprising what can be done on the PC; even the large design and advertising agencies now use PCs to produce much of their materials!

You may even find that your clients respond to the fact that you don't spend large sums on promotional material; it can become a talking point that you use technology pragmatically and effectively and keep your costs down.

Another advantage of doing it yourself is that you can tailor promotional material for particular customers, for example brochures that target particular industry sectors or types of client. If your business requires you to make presentations, for instance, pitching for new work or a conference talk, you can produce overhead projection slides specifically for it. Furthermore, the preparation can be left to the last minute as you are not dependent on external companies.

All this can be achieved using your PC, a high quality printer and software that allows you to produce the materials. If you are mostly only concerned with producing textual information, you could simply use a word-processor. On the other hand, reports, letter-headings, overhead projection slides, etc, can be greatly enhanced by the inclusion of graphics to help put points simply and convey a good impression. There are many presentation graphics software packages available. Using a laser or colour ink-jet printer you can print them on to plain paper or acetate sheets for overhead projection slides. Alternatively, you can send the data file to a bureau service to produce 35mm colour slides. Furthermore, most word-processing packages allow you to load the data prepared by the presentation graphics package for inclusion into reports.

If you are heavily involved in the design industry and regularly produce detailed written materials that involve complex design and layout, it may also be worth considering a desktop publishing software package (DTP). Such software has been designed to enable professional typesetting on a PC. However, for most home-based businesses, where it is likely that you will in any case use word-processing software, it is probably more economical to buy a presentation graphics package that will enhance your word-processing facility. It is common (and cost-effective) nowadays to buy what it is called an 'Office Package' which combines word-processing, presentation graphics, database and spread-sheet software in a single package and which usually does not cost a lot more than the individual pieces of software on their own.

Presentation graphics software

In Chapter 8 I described how spreadsheet software can be regarded as the numerical equivalent of word-processing. In the same way presentation graphics software is the graphics equivalent. It allows you to produce drawings, charts and diagrams by providing you with an electronic drawing tool. The software is best used with the aid of an additional piece of hardware called a mouse, which plugs into the back of the PC and complements the keyboard. The mouse is a small device that you can move on your desk and it controls a pointer on the screen. You can use the mouse to select items from a menu on the screen and to help you draw shapes such as lines, boxes and circles, enabling you to produce detailed illustrations.

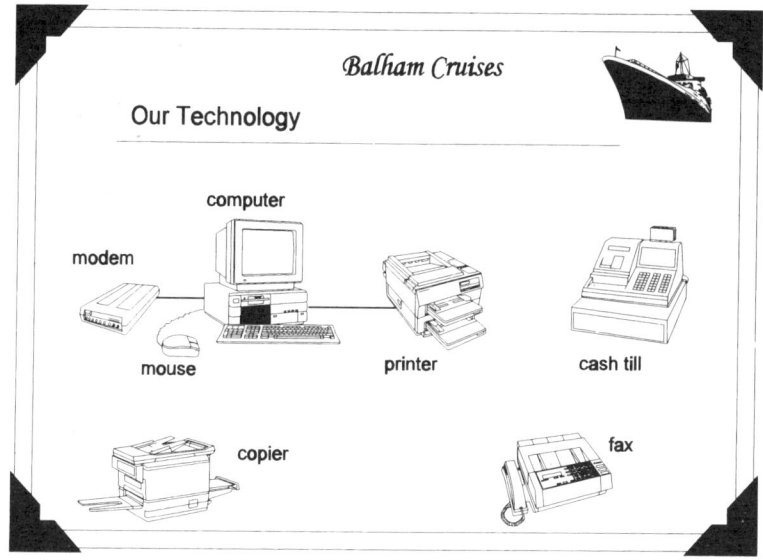

Figure 9.1 *Typical clip-art images*

To make it easier and quicker, presentation graphics software usually includes many more facilities to help with constructing drawings, such as a wide range of clip-art drawings. Figure 9.1 illustrates typical clip-art images – PC, fax, photocopier, modem, mouse, cash-till – even the border. These drawings can be positioned on the screen wherever you like and scaled to whatever size you want. A whole series of other options (too numerous to mention) exists to help you create your own personalised drawings, including the ability to add text (with different font sizes, styles and appearance), rotate images, superimpose other images and draw freehand.

Once a drawing is finished, it can be printed. The printer that you use for your word-processing will usually be able to print out the graphics; however, for the best quality and highest speed, a laser printer is really needed. Most people do not have high-quality colour printers, but low-cost types are available (such as the colour bubble-jet printers) which will enable you to make good use of the colour capability of presentation graphics software.

Price range
Presentation graphics software
£60 – £300

Letter-headings and with-compliments slips

If you are not bothered by the inclusion of colour in your business literature you can save on printing bills by doing it all on your PC. Furthermore, you can prepare all your literature using your word-processor. The simplicity of letter-headings and with-compliments slips that purely state the business name, address, telephone and fax numbers, using a single font in different sizes, is often the most effective: in fact, one of the most prominent corporate identity companies does just this on their own letter-headings.

When using the word-processor, you can store a template of your letter-heading and retrieve this each time you write a letter, so the heading is printed with the letter itself. Alternatively, you can use a feature of the word-processor called a macro facility, which enables you to record a series of key-strokes and then 'play' them back – similar to recording and playing back music on tape. The key-strokes would typically include your business name, address, telephone and fax numbers together with codes for their positioning on the paper and the size of the fonts. You can also include a code to print the correct date automatically. This means that when you want to type a letter, all you need do is 'play-back' the series of key-strokes (by feeding in a code) and the dated letter-heading is ready for you to write the letter.

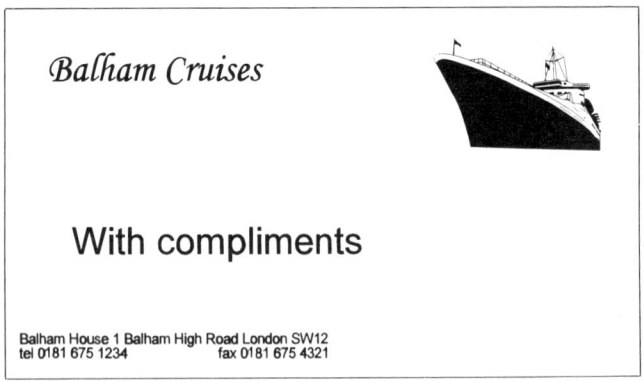

Figure 9.2 *Typical with-compliments slip*

A logo or any other graphic can be included in this letter-heading and the presentation graphics software can be used to prepare the logo. Once drawn, the same process described above (using the word-processor macro facility) can be followed, modified to include keystrokes to position the logo where you want it.

The same process can be used to prepare other literature, for instance invoices, purchase orders, forms, statements – using a different code to 'call-up' the relevant document.

In the same way you can prepare with-compliments slips (see Figure 9.2) and print these out in bulk with three to an A4 page; they can be cut up using a guillotine.

Business cards and report covers

Unlike letter headings and with-compliments slips, it is not possible to print business cards and report covers on most types of printer (they will not be able to handle the thickness of the card), so this is one item where you have to visit the printers. However, you can typeset the material, enabling you to keep the same style as your other literature. Again, this can be achieved using the word-processor alone or in conjunction with the presentation graphics package (Figure 9.3 illustrates a typical business card produced in this way). It is usually best to visit the printers first and ask them how they want you to produce the copy. They will either ask for what they call 'camera-ready copy' and tell you what type of paper to use for this (some papers are better than others) or some printers will be able to take your data file (eg delivered on a floppy disc) and print from this.

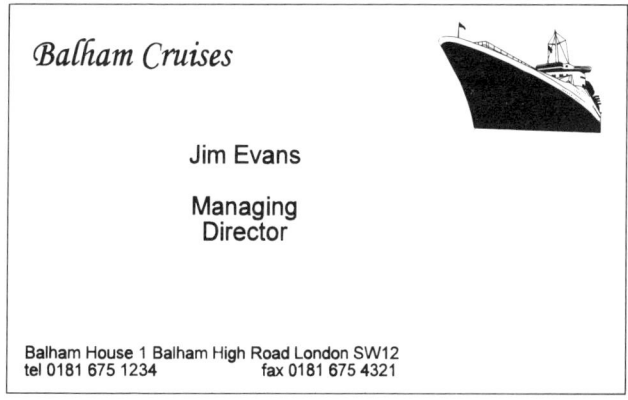

Balham Cruises

Jim Evans

Managing
Director

Balham House 1 Balham High Road London SW12
tel 0181 675 1234   fax 0181 675 4321

Figure 9.3 *Business card*

Typical printing prices
Business cards £25 per 250
Report covers £50 per 250

Proposals, reports

A good word-processing package is the most appropriate tool for preparing proposals and reports, combined with a high-quality printer.

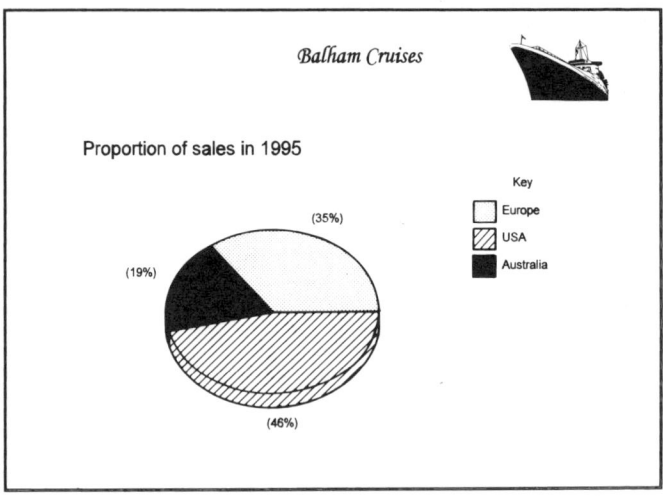

Figure 9.4 *Pie chart*

However, you can improve the look of your proposals and reports by the addition of graphics. For instance, you may want to include charts or diagrams to help explain complex messages (see Figure 9.4). People are much more likely to focus their attention on these and pick up on key points.

You can create such illustrations using presentation graphics software and then incorporate these into the word-processed document, positioning them wherever you like in the document.

Most stationers will provide a binding service to bind your reports and proposals, but if you want to have this facility in your home, you can purchase binding machines which can handle up to 200-page documents for as little as £120. It is possible to buy cheaper ones if your documents are not going to exceed 25 pages.

Overhead projection slides

Paper is not the only medium on which you can print. Most good business stationers will supply transparent acetate paper for use with high-quality printers, though if you have a laser printer, you must use special sheets that can withstand the heat of the printing process, otherwise you could wreck the printer. All you need do is to insert the acetate paper into the laser printer instead of your ordinary paper and print in the normal way (see Figure 9.5).

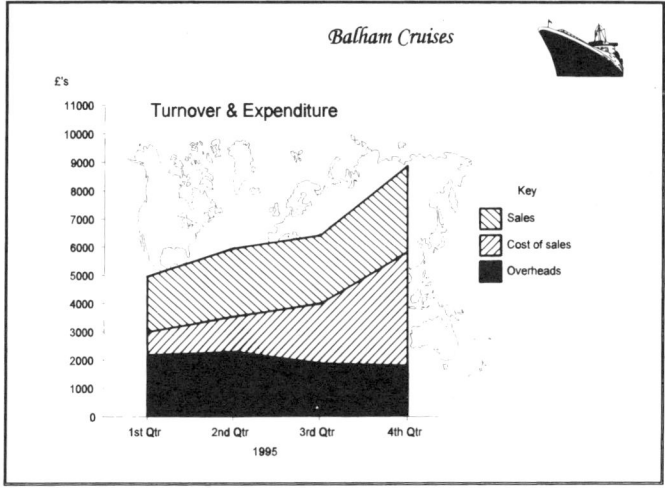

Figure 9.5 *Graphic for overhead projection slide*

It is also possible to buy the mountings on which to mount the acetate paper.

If you need colour in your overhead projection slides, you can either buy a colour printer or, if this is not a frequent requirement, you can use one of the growing number of bureau services. You send them the data file on a floppy disc and they will produce colour acetate copies for you (most presentation graphics software allows you to draw in colour), usually by return of post.

The best way of finding out your nearest bureau service is to contact the supplier of your presentation graphics software package. They usually keep a list of companies who are familiar with your particular software package. Alternatively, let your fingers do the talking with *Yellow Pages*.

35mm colour slides

In the same way that you can send bureau services a data file for producing overhead projection slides, you can also use the service to produce 35mm slides, again, usually by return of post. The slides produced are high quality and, one of the benefits of producing them on your own PC is that you can also print them out (in black and white) on your own printer, or include them in a proposal or report (see Figure 9.6).

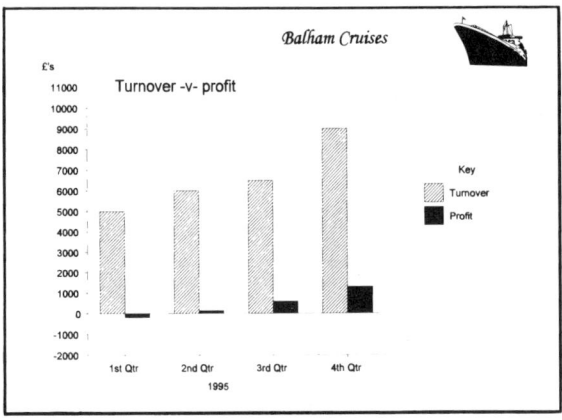

Figure 9.6   *35mm slide print-out*

Promotional material

How you prepare this material very much depends upon how much you want to spend and the quality of the final material. If cost is a major issue, there is no reason why you cannot prepare material using a combination of word-processing and presentation graphics software and print them on your own laser printer. You will be limited to black and white material, though you can use coloured paper to make them that little bit different from ordinary reports. If you have the luxury of a colour printer, it is possible to print very effective material. Alternatively, you can use a bureau service to bulk print your flyers (which could contain colour content) by sending them the data file in the same way you would do for 35mm slides. Indeed, there is a cut-off point where it is cheaper to go to the printers than use your own printer.

Multi-page brochures can be prepared in the same way and then bound using a binding machine. This can be cost effective provided you do not want to produce large numbers of brochures. It also has the advantage that you can tailor them to suit specific requirements, either a particular customer or market sector. If, however, you need to produce just one high-quality brochure in bulk, it is probably better to use the printers, and produce the basic copy for this on your PC. The brochures can then be printed on to high-quality card. There is a whole range of options you can include, from simple two-colour to a full colour brochure, depending upon the quality you want and the money you are prepared to spend. A good printing company or bureau service will talk over all the options with you.

Hand drawings

There may well be times where you want to include hand drawings in your reports, slides or promotional material – in other words, artwork that has not been prepared on a PC. To do this, you will need to buy a scanning machine which will allow you to scan the drawing and store it as an image data file on your PC. Most presentation graphics packages and word-processing packages then allow you to include this drawing as part of your artwork. Figure 9.7 shows an example of this – a black and white cartoon.

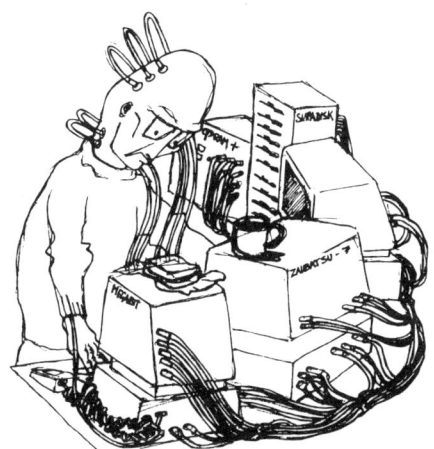

Figure 9.7 *Scanned image of a cartoon*

Scanners are not too expensive to buy, though the alternative is to use a bureau service which will scan your drawing and provide you with a data file on a floppy disc.

Scanner price range
Hand scanners £60 – £150
Flat-bed scanners £150 – £1500

Kodak Photo-CD

The Kodak Photo-CD service is a very useful means of converting high quality 35mm slides and negatives into a graphics format that will enable you to incorporate the pictures into your graphics presentation, word-processing or desktop publishing files. All you need do is to take your slides or negatives into your nearest high-street photographic shop that operates the service and within one or two weeks they will return a Photo-CD – a CD-ROM with the pictures stored as graphics files. You will need a CD-ROM drive that can read the Photo-CD and a graphics presentation software that is compatible with Photo-CD. The service is not that much more expensive than ordinary film processing and can therefore be a cost-effective means of converting pictures into a form suitable for displaying on your PC. The CD-ROM can also be played on a number of different consumer electronics devices such as the Philips CD-I (compact disc interactive) player, enabling you to display the slides on your TV.

Digital cameras

An alternative to scanning pictures is to buy one of the new digital cameras. These look similar to ordinary cameras but instead of storing pictures on ordinary film, they store them as digital files which can be transferred to your PC. You can then include the pictures in presentation materials and reports, just as if you had scanned a picture. This is a lot quicker than taking pictures using an ordinary camera, having them developed and printed and then scanned.

Prices of digital cameras
£300 – £700

Your business identity

When presented with all these technology tools, that help you to produce high quality written materials, it is tempting to think that this will automatically make a graphic designer out of you.

Certainly, the flexibility of the PC allows you easily to try out different combinations of fonts, layout, text sizes and so on. But unless you have a particular flair for graphic design, you will probably still benefit from good advice as to how you can prepare really polished material. Furthermore, it is easy to forget the need for a consistent and unique style in the materials that you use in your business. Remember that all the materials you produce are saying something about your business – giving it an image – and if your letter-headings, business cards and promotional material all use different fonts and sizes of text, it will not give the impression to your clients of a 'solid' and well established business.

It can be worth while to take advice from an expert graphic designer as to the look and feel of the materials you produce – another home-based business owner perhaps? You could produce the basic details of your materials on your own PC and send the designer the data files, to which he can add the design touch. He is also likely to make sure that there is a consistency to all your materials, so that the business cards, letter-headings, with-compliments slips, report covers, brochures and so on all have the same look and feel.

In this way, your promotional material will have a professional look with minimal expenditure.

10

Choosing and maintaining your personal computer

If you ask a cross-section of PC users what type you should buy, you will get a wide range of firm opinions. It's rather like asking for opinions when buying a car: what you hear is usually based on experience, familiarity and prejudice, rather than on impartial comment. That is why it is an extremely good idea to talk to a whole number of people, to get different perspectives.

Deciding what type (standard) of PC to buy must be carefully thought out as this will dictate issues such as how easy it is to use, the range of possible software applications, its flexibility, compatibility with other PCs and costs.

In the early days of the PC there was a whole range of different standards and makes to choose from, mostly incompatible with each other, causing great confusion among users. When IBM entered the PC market, they brought with them an industry standard around which software developers could be sure of a stable hardware device on which they could base their products. The IBM standard has been much criticised by computer people for its lack of technical performance, though these people are not always aware of the need for standards – if they had their way, we would be changing our computers every year to keep up with technological advances. As it is, it has broadly been possible to upgrade your PC to more powerful ones, without having to change your applications software or your data files.

The IBM Personal Computer standard remains the most common throughout the UK business world, though there is another personal computer standard – the Apple Mac – that is also common. (Strictly speaking, 'Personal Computer' and 'PC' are trademarks of IBM, though throughout this book 'PC' is used in its broadest sense to include any personal computer.) Unfortunately, the two types of standard are at present mostly incompatible with each other.

Traditionally, the Apple Mac has been favoured by users who want a personal computer that is simple to operate as it adopts a graphics-based screen design which is consistent throughout all its software; this saves users having to learn different command structures for different software. The downside to this is that Apple personal computers have always been more expensive to buy than IBM ones – and this has been one of the chief reasons why Apple Macs are not so commonly used, particularly in the UK. However, Apple are learning from IBM on this one and are increasingly making their computers cheaper.

There are two other reasons why the IBM standard PC is more widespread. First, it is far more flexible than the Apple for connecting third-party hardware and applications software, and this has meant that a large worldwide industry has grown for the supply of these add-ons, enabling prices to be kept low. Second, although IBM set the standard, you do not have to buy from IBM; there is a large range of cheap clones – other manufacturers' PCs – all much the same as the IBM model. *There's nothing like competition to keep the prices low!*

When the IBM PC first came out, unlike the Apple Mac, it did not use a graphics-based screen design. Instead you had to type commands in from the keyboard, which most non-technical people and those with no typing skills found difficult to use. Furthermore, there was no control over the design of software applications by different companies, leading to great inconsistency in the command structures of how they were used. This meant that if you bought a number of different software applications (word-processing, spreadsheet, database etc), they all had a different style of commands and these had to be learnt each time. This has since changed and most IBM standard PCs are now purchased with a software system called Windows (a trademark of MicroSoft Corporation) that provides much the same functionality as with Apple Macs – a graphics-based screen design that software applications are designed to comply with (there are different versions of Windows, the most common being Windows 3.1, Windows for Workgroups and Windows '95. At the time of going to press, Windows '95 is the most recent version and it is usually best to buy your PC with the most recent version pre-installed). It's rather like cars; when you switch from one car to another you don't want to have to learn a whole new set of controls each time (we have all managed at some time to turn the windscreen wipers on just when we were intending to turn left) and car manufacturers are gradually realising this and are trying to bring some consistency to the controls.

It is even the case now that, although IBM and Apple personal computers are mostly incompatible with each other, a few software developers are designing their software (eg word-processing) so that the data files prepared on an IBM PC can be transferred on to an Apple Mac and vice versa. In other words, as time moves on, the difference between the IBM and Apple standards is narrowing, on features such as ease of use, cost and flexibility. Furthermore, Apple have now made moves to allow other manufacturers to clone their machines and are introducing a new feature to some of their personal computers that will allow them to emulate the IBM standard. While on the surface this could give the best of both worlds, in practice there is a price premium to pay for this.

The most important thing to remember is, if you are working with other people – either clients, suppliers or colleagues – it makes sense to keep to the same standard of PC, so that you can use compatible software and easily exchange data files with each other. This is particularly important in the design world; if your business involves using a personal computer to design artwork using desktop publishing and presentation graphics packages, it is probably best to stick to the Apple Mac as most printers and bureau services use Apples. If not, my personal preference is to stick to the IBM standard as it is the most widely used throughout the UK (and world). Other reasons for this choice include cost, flexibility and compatibility with the vast majority of my clients' systems. If you get confused by all this, don't worry too much. Even in big corporations, you hear everyday discussions as to whether the IBM or Apple standard should be used.

Portable or desktop PC?

Having chosen the type or standard of computer, the next choice is whether you want a portable or desktop machine. If frequent travel is not a feature of your business, a desktop machine is probably the most suitable. Like for like, they are cheaper than portable machines. Furthermore, the screens are easier to read, particularly if you will be working long hours with them and it is easier to position the screen and keyboard into a comfortable position for working long hours. They also offer more possibilities for connecting peripheral devices.

If, however, you need to carry a computer around with you, a portable model can be an ideal choice, allowing you to work anywhere. The smallest and lightest practical machines are called notebook computers. They are about the size of an A4 sheet in cross section and can fit in a briefcase. They are even powered by rechargeable batteries so that you can have up to three hours of usage without a recharge, though if you need to carry the charger for the battery pack with you, it can be quite a hefty item – salesmen are not always keen to show you this until you've bought the machine!

Portable models will typically include options for:

- Incorporating a modem and fax facility, either built-in or external to the body, allowing you to communicate with other people – wherever you are
- Connecting a portable printer
- Connecting a mouse
- Connecting an external screen and keyboard to make typing and viewing the screen less of a strain.

Technical feature specification

The specification for the various technical features of your computer will be determined by the software applications that you will use. Items to consider are:

- *The hard disc storage space:* this will be dictated by how many software packages you have, the storage space they require and how much data you are likely to generate. If you are going to generate multimedia data (eg voice and video files), these take up large quantities of space and many software programs themselves are 'byte guzzlers'. It is usually best therefore to over-specify your hard disc size, allowing for room to grow.
- *The computer memory (RAM):* this will be dictated by the applications software requirements. If you don't have enough memory for your applications, it will slow them down and even possibly not allow them to run. Plenty of memory is important if you are using presentation graphics and desktop publishing software. You can, however, upgrade the PC's memory at a later date if you find this becomes necessary.
- *The computer processor speed:* basically how fast the computer operates. If you are using simple word-processing, the speed is not too critical; however, if you are going to use presentation graphics or desktop publishing software you will need a high-speed machine.
- *The expandability:* how many peripheral devices the personal computer can connect.

- *Graphics card:* your PC connects to its screen via a graphics card. Ensure that you have one of the high-speed type, for example PCI.
- *Up-gradability:* can the computer's processor be up-graded to run faster?
- *Compatibility with chosen software and peripheral hardware.*

Multimedia

Many new PCs can be purchased with a multimedia capability as a standard feature included in the price. This usually means that it will include a sound (expansion) card, an amplifier and loudspeakers, a CD-ROM drive and software called Video for Windows that will allow your PC to display video.

The sound card fits into the expansion slots of the PC and all you will need to do is to connect a lead from the card (usually at the back of the PC) into the amplifier and then connect the loudspeakers to the amplifier. Software will be provided which will allow you to record and play back sound just like a tape recorder, except that the sound is recorded on to the PC's hard disc. The sound you record can be from a microphone, an ordinary tape recorder, or any other sound device.

The CD-ROM drive will most likely be located near to the floppy disc drive and will allow you to insert published CD-ROMs in a similar way to inserting floppy discs. An example of an interactive multimedia CD-ROM is MicroSoft's encyclopedia called *Encarta*. This is, in effect, a multimedia database that includes text, graphics, animations, music, voice and video information. You can explore the database in a number of different ways. For instance, you can search the database for all references to Stravinsky and then hear a selection of his music. Similarly, you could search the database for references to the Hubble space telescope and then see a video showing how it was repaired. The video that you see will be displayed in a small window on the screen, though it will not be of the highest quality.

If you want to upgrade your existing PC with a multimedia capability, all of the above options can be purchased separately. You will need to install these yourself and this is not usually a straightforward task. However, a few manufactures sell a complete multimedia kit which is a sensible option to choose as the various elements have been designed to work together and such kits usually represent good value for money. If you are unfamiliar with installing such devices, it is probably better to get an expert to do this for you. You can always watch and learn from how it is done.

Sound cards are a much of a muchness, rather like buying hi-fi – the only differences tend to be if you want some advanced sound recording and editing features. However, the purchase of a CD-ROM drive needs a little more attention to the following requirements:

- *Speed.* You should make sure that your CD-ROM drive, at the very minimum, is a quad speed drive and, preferably, faster, such as x6 or x8. This refers to how fast the PC finds and retrieves information off the CD-ROM, which is particularly important for video.
- *Standard.* Not all CD-ROM drives are of the same technical capabilities when it comes to being multimedia compliant. The more recent types of drive can play the full range of multimedia information and they are referred to as 'white-book' compatible. You should therefore ensure that any CD-ROM purchased either on its own or in a new PC complies with this standard.
- *Internal or external.* CD-ROM drives that come ready installed in new PCs are usually of the internal variety, fitted into the chassis of the PC. If you are buying a CD-ROM drive separately, you have the option of choosing an internal or external drive. It is usually neater to install the internal drive option into the PC; however, this can be a fiddly job. External drives save this bother and can be connected to the PC either via the printer connector or via a separate expansion card that you will need to install into the PC.

Multimedia costs
Multimedia kit: £150 – £400
(sound card, amplifier, loudspeakers, CD-ROM)

Many other multimedia 'toys' can be purchased, though it is questionable whether these should be considered as essentials for the home office. Examples are:

- *TV tuner:* an expansion card that allows you to watch TV on your screen.
- *MPEG card:* an expansion card that allows you to play the new video CDs on your PC with a quality the same or better than from a VHS cassette (video CDs store approximately 60 minutes' worth of high-quality film on a compact disc and are usually played on devices such as a Philips CD-I player – compact disc interactive).
- *Music keyboard:* a piano-type keyboard that will plug into your PC (eg via the sound card) to allow you to record music on to the hard disc and compose multi-part music.

- *Video capture card:* an expansion card that allows you to record video on to your hard disc from devices such as a CamCorder or VHS cassette recorder.

Some people regard multimedia as being rather a gimmick and of no use to the home-based business. While this has been true in the past, there is gradually emerging a large range of multimedia publications which can be extremely useful. Many software packages are now sold and distributed on a CD-ROM, complete with a multimedia training package to help you to learn quickly. Such training packages guide you through how the software can be used and typically include a soundtrack, animations and sometimes video to add clarity. Such training packages are not limited to the subject of computer software and many other areas are now covered, including language training and personal and technical skills training, representing a cost-effective way of developing your skills and capabilities.

If you are really adventurous, you can even include multimedia information in your presentations that you develop either using graphics presentation software or special multimedia authoring software. Such software allows you to include sound, still pictures and moving video into your presentations.

Choosing a printer

Choosing a printer is rather like choosing any technical item; it is mostly a trade-off between performance, quality and price. For instance, if you were buying a camera, you might want to take high-quality indoor portrait shots (using a number of different lenses) as well as having a camera to take with you for snaps when rock-climbing. With such a broad need, you might be better off having two separate cameras – a light portable cheap one for the snaps (it doesn't matter too much if it gets damaged) and an expensive quality camera for the indoor portraits. Alternatively, you could buy a single camera that represents a more cost-effective compromise between the two diverse needs. In other words, it is all about trade-offs between price, performance and quality.

It is much the same with printers, which, for word-processing purposes, can be divided into three main types:

- Dot matrix
- Ink-jet
- Laser.

The *dot matrix* has been around the longest, and has secured a reputation for reliability, cheapness and versatility. It fires a matrix of pins through a ribbon on to paper, moving from one character to the next across a page. You will typically encounter 9-pin or 24-pin options – the more pins, the greater the quality of text. Such printers will also work with multi-part stationery; for instance, if you are printing accounts information – pre-printed invoices, statements, etc – you can print carbon copies automatically. They also commonly come in both A4 and A3 size and in portable versions. The disadvantages are that they can be noisy and slow and do not produce the excellent print quality of the ink-jet or laser printers. Nowadays, the ink-jet printer has mostly replaced the dot matrix printer as the preferred low-cost printer choice.

Ink-jet printers overcome some of the problems of dot-matrix printers. They are low-noise and the print quality is good, though they are more expensive than dot-matrix printers. They work on the principle of spraying ink through small nozzles on to paper; however, this can lead to some problems – if the correct paper is not used, the ink can take some time to dry, and, if handled, will blot. Furthermore, this can lead to some unreliability problems if the ink gets clogged in the jets. Having said this, the manufacturers are improving quality and reliability, and these printers can represent excellent value for money. They are available in either A4 or A3 size, in colour versions and as portable models, which are particularly useful for use with notebook or portable computers. But beware, the portable models are not always as portable as you think; once you include the power pack and the sheet-feeder, they can get quite bulky.

At the top end of the scale are laser printers which feature excellent print quality combined with low noise and high speed. These printers are a must if you need to produce quality documents. They also have the greatest versatility for including different typefaces and fonts, and printing illustrations and drawings. The main disadvantages are that they are more expensive to buy and operate than dot matrix and ink-jet printers and they are heavy machines, preventing them from being carried around with a portable or notebook computer.

Laser printers work on the principle of pulses of laser light forming a pattern of dots on to an electrostatic drum – which, in turn, is translated on to paper. The number of dots per inch (rather like the dot-matrix printer) reflects the print quality and is typically 300 dpi (dots per inch). The lasers use toner in this process, which needs renewing every so often. The cost of toner (or an alternative cheaper method, having your toner cartridges refilled) will be more expensive

Printer	Paper sizes	Paper handling	Print quality	Speed	Noise	Colour content	Graphics capability	Purchase cost	Operating costs	Portability
Dot-matrix	Either A4 or A3 sizes commonly available	Multi-part stationery, carbon copies, envelopes, labels	Low to medium quality	Low to medium speed	High	Available	Yes	Low to medium	Low	Versions available
Ink-Jet	Mostly A4, some A3 sizes available	Single-part stationery only, envelopes, labels,	Medium to high quality (but can be problems with ink drying)	Medium speed	Low	Available	Yes	Medium	Average	Versions available
Laser	Up to A4 mostly - A3 sizes exist but very expensive	Single-part stationery only, envelopes, labels	High quality	High speed	Low	Only available in very expensive machines	Yes	High	High	No portable versions available

Table 10.1 *Main types of printer for word processors*

than the ribbon and ink-jet refills for the dot-matrix and ink-jet printers, though ink-jet refills require changing more frequently.

Laser printers are particularly useful if you want a variety of typefaces and graphics included in documents. The manufacturers work on the principle that the bottom of the range model is the cheapest, but tend to put a high price on additions such as font cartridges and fast printing. Other additions typically include two-bin trays – useful if you use different types of paper – and double-sided printing. Table 10.1 provides a summary of the main types of printer.

Printer price range
Dot matrix £80 – £500
Ink-jet £100 – £800
Laser £250 – £5000

Buying a printer is in some ways much easier than buying software. You can see a printer being demonstrated, see the print quality, the different typefaces and fonts, the graphics capability, the speed etc. This can be done by going into shops and asking for demonstrations.

Maintaining your PC

The cynics among us will read much of this book with reservations about the use of technology – what happens when it goes wrong, either through breakdown or operator error? Such sentiments are certainly healthy, but they must be looked at in proportion. Most technology tools are very reliable these days, through manufacturers' keen attention to quality control. But there will be times when you get problems, often at moments when you need them least. When you first start using technology, this might not be too critical, but as time goes on, your business will become increasingly dependent upon it. Because of its generally good record on reliability, it is easy to get lulled into a false sense of security. It is very important to plan for such events in order to minimise the damage that can be caused. For instance, your fax machine may break down, just when you are expecting important documents to come through, or your PC's hard disc may suddenly 'crash' and lose your valuable data – what if you haven't got back-up copies of your data?

Furthermore, you may cause the problem yourself. Suppose you are working on a long document over a period of a day and forget to save it regularly on to the hard disc – a power failure will give rise to some colourful language!

WORKING AT HOME OR LIVING AT WORK?

The Microsoft guide to getting the balance right.

Files snaking across the bedroom floor and client records mingling with the coffee cups on the kitchen bench are sometimes unavoidable when you work at home but, there's a fine line between working at home and living at work. If you allow too much overlap between home and office space, your performance in the former and your ability to relax in the latter will both be the worse for it.

According to the pundits, if you have set up an office in the house, you have moved to SoHo-land (Small Office/Home Office : hence, SoHo). The ideal SoHo solution is to have your main office systems - for business planning, writing, printing letters, filing, analysing your sales figures, doing the books, communicating with clients and others - all on one desktop.

This beats having a typewriter and all its resulting paper files in one corner, an accounting system that takes over the dining room table, paper business plan projections stuck all over the walls and a sea of client information surrounding the phone in the hall.

The problem was that, until recently, software packages designed to allow you to carry out the key elements of home-business activity together in an integrated way simply did not exist. In recent years Microsoft, the company responsible for the world's best selling small business software, has developed a package that brings together all the main office functions on one desktop, with the price and performance needs of the home-office in mind. So, taming the home-office and confining it to the desktop is finally possible.

Where Does Windows 95 Fit in?

UNless you live on Mars, you can't have missed the fanfare surrounding the Microsoft Windows 95 launch. This is a piece of software, known as the operating system, that helps you run the word processor, spreadsheet and other business tools installed on your PC. Windows 95 is the next generation of the Windows operating system, the standard operating system for the majority of the world's personal computers, both in business and at home.

PCs used to be single station, isolated systems. But, increasingly, business is about connecting. Windows 95 makes it easy to link your PC to other computers via phone lines or over the Internet, by adding a modem (a box that links your PC to the phone line). Microsoft Windows 95 gives you more power on your desktop than ever before. Above all, its easy-to-use features mean getting started and configuring your PC is simpler, perfect for anyone who hasn't quite mastered the intricacies of IT management! Everyday tasks will suddenly be accomplished more quickly and with far greater ease and, with the ability to perform different tasks at the same time, you'll have more time to actually run your business.

Microsoft Office has become the world's most popular office software suite, with an installed base of twenty two million worldwide. Microsoft Office application provide essential business tools for the more sophisticated user without sacrificing ease-of-use. Office provides more options for the business user but has Microsoft's IntelliSense technology built in to guide users through more complex tasks. Businesses that need to manipulate and analyse complex information or that may want to customise the software find Office a particularly close fit to their needs.

Microsoft Office Professional for Windows 95 includes:

- Microsoft Word for word processing
- Microsoft Excel for spreadsheet work
- PowerPoint for presentation graphics
- Schedule + for time management
- Access for Windows, the easy to use database application

One of the main reasons for the popularity of Microsoft Office is seamless integration of the entire package. Each separate part of Microsoft Office is designed to be easy to use with the other elements of the package. For example, using the 'drag and drop' facility, transferring information from Excel to a chart in PowerPoint is simple and instead of spending valuable time retyping client information from the database into Word documents, the data can be moved across with one quick key stroke.

Microsoft Office Tools in Action: The Consultancy Group

Established 5 years ago, The Consultancy Group are a firm of financial planners specialising in putting together portfolios for professional couples and those who have recently retired although their client base is moving further towards private individuals with their own small business. The firm has a staff of eight and each has a PC running Microsoft Windows 95 and Office Professional.

Michael Hauge, a partner in the firm, explains that they were attempting to build up the firm's system gradually. "However, with the advent of Microsoft Windows 95 we decided to follow a deliberate policy to move to the new application and have everything Microsoft based. Running a single operating system helped us remove some of the real headaches that technology can cause. Integration is no longer a problem, support is much easier, and the different applications are less likely to argue!"

Michael thinks that The Consultancy Group is well on the way to achieving the 'paperless office'. "Everything is on email now so messages no longer get lost and as we can fax documents straight from PCs, we don't waste valuable time standing over the fax machines. If we need to get a specialised quote from a number of different organisations, we simply punch in 12 numbers to our PCs and 12 faxes get sent to various points across the country."

> "We were considering spending £15,000 on a document management system but we got part of it for nothing when we installed Windows 95," explained MIchael. "It also allows us to hook up to the Internet and utilise all the information available there. Its strange but, although we've always relied heavily on technology and have grown steadily over the last five years, due to the speed of the machines and the networks, and the usability of the software, we actually find ourselves with fewer machines than we had this time last year."

Word for Windows is the best-selling word processing package in the world. As well as its ease of use, one of the features that has helped make Word a best seller throughout the world is its ability to automate tasks, such as direct mail shots, mail merges and setting up letter and fax templates. With so many of these tasks delegated to the system itself, the user can now exploit the word processor to the full with less cost in terms of hours spent at their machine.

Microsoft Excel is also a best-selling application and is the most popular spre adsheet in the world. As well as guiding you through some of the more complex tasks, the latest versions of Excel even 'read' how you are using them and alert you with personalised tips on shortcuts or features you are not using that could make you more productive! For instance, its AutoComplete feature zips through repetitive data entry in columns by automatically completing an entry for you as the first few letters are typed.

Office 95 is designed with small business users in mind. If you setting up a business from home, chances are that you won't have the time to spend hours looking through manuals on how to make the software work best for you. In answer to the specialised needs of a small enterprise, Office now offers the next generation of IntelliSense technology which has been designed to enable easy access to the full power of your tools. To learn how to perform a new task simply ask the Answer Wizard a question in your own words and it will give you the answer you need instantly. Another example of IntellSense is Excel's Chart Wizard which makes it easy to create great looking charts from scratch.

Microsoft realises that professional-looking presentations are becoming more important in winning and maintaining business, and Power Point's unbeatable graphics' ability is widely-rated as the most effective tool for creating eye-catching presentations that win arguments.

MIcrosoft Office also includes an easy to use database called Access for Windows. Access imports data from many other sources so you don't have to re-enter your data to get started. Access has been specifically designed to make it easy for database novices. Microsoft Access lets you use existing spreadsheet data, or you can use its built-in database Wizard to prepare a new database from a selection of templates, giving you the answer you need at the touch of a button.

Finally, Schedule+ makes it easy to organise your day, week or month as well as keeping track of projects, assignments and all your key contacts. Allowing you to view all your appointments, manage key contacts and keep on top of all your tasks, Schedule+ helps you manage your time more efficiently and even helps you work more effectively with others by utilising the group scheduling function.

Microsoft Office Tools in Action: The Asset Manager's Tale

Daniel L Lieberman Esq was established in 1986 as a family business, with three employees and three PCs. Daniel Lieberman describes his business at "the management of clients' assets in securities, bonds and real estate", with most of the company's clients based in the United States.

Among other software tools, the firm's three PCs run the powerful Microsoft Access database and the ·best-selling Excel spreadsheet system, both of which are available as part of the integrated Microsoft Office package. MS Office is designed particularly for experienced PC users and is commonly chosen by firms with a need for a suite of office tools which combine power with flexibility.

The Access database is used by the Lieberman family firm to hold and provide access to data on securities, including details such as when coupons are payable or have matured or are due for replacement. Similarly, the firm uses Excel spreadsheets to present statistical information for analytical purpose. Excel provides the capability to design spreadsheets to match a particular firm's exact needs and Mrs. Lieberman, who handles much of the family company's business administration, uses it to design spreadsheets that make sense of the complex statistics involved in securities and bond management.

The Liebermans' applications software runs on the Windows 95 operating system (see Windows 95 box), which makes it easy to link a PC to the Internet via a modem. The firm has linked up two PCs in this way, enabling them to action buy and sell decisions electronically and giving access to a wealth of business information to inform the decision-making. "Financial savings have come as a result of timely information made possible by Microsoft and linkage to the Internet", commented Daniel Lieberman.

Microsoft Office first defined the office suite and continues to do so. Office Professional for Windows 95 allows someone starting up on their own for the first time the flexibility to run the business the way they want it to run. No longer will important meetings be missed amongst piles of paper and forgetting to call clients because their number is underneath all of the unpaid invoices will become a thing of the past. Microsoft Office Professional for Windows 95 frees you to focus on the most important job of all - getting your job done.

For more information on MS Office, Windows 95, ask your local PC dealer.

"HOME OFFICE" – A COMPI

Many homes do not have the space available for a modern office workstation. Grahl have introduced the **HOME OFFICE** which provides a complete office within as little floor space as 6.5ft^2. The two styles of desks which are built within a cupboard have been ergonomically designed for ease of use even in rooms with limited space.

HOME OFFICE cupboards each incorporate levelling adjustments at all four corners and height adjustable work surfaces are an option. Ampl storage is provide within the pedestals an the units are designed ensure adequate spac for computer monito system unit, keyboar and mouse as well as fax and telephon Cable management fac lities a available an cable acce ports can b easily cut in the bac walls. A wid variety o finishes en ables a close match t existing home furn ture, whilst the choic in widths, heights an add-on shelving uni

E OFFICE IN A CUPBOARD

elps to fit **HOME OFFICE** into even the mallest rooms.

Also illustrated ithin the photograph ; a chair from our YNCHRON DUO-ACK range

f seating. he unique lugger UO-BACK as been de-eloped by eloped by rahl to pro-ide greater comfort to ndividuals with seden-ary or static job nctions, thus reducing bsenteeism from work hrough back, neck and houlder conditions. he unique split back ads of the backrest

encourage the user to sit posturally correctly and therefore more healthily, enabling higher levels of concentration to be maintained. The **DUO-BACK** supports the back and en-courages con-stant shifts in posture.

For further information on **HOME OFFICE** and the **DUO-BACK** range of seating, please con-tact Grahl UK Limited, Unit 12, Chiltern Court, Asheridge Road, Chesham, Bucks, HP5 2PX.
Tel: 01494/792601.
Fax: 01494/792936.

THE⚜EXPRESS

NEW Titles from The Express series

Your Home Office
Third Edition
Peter Chatterton

If you plan to run a business from home or use a room there for occasional freelance work, you will need a copy of **Your Home Office**.

It describes how to choose and set up an office that will enable you to work efficiently, productively and profitably. Topics covered include:

◆ what basic equipment can provide the facilities of a modern office

◆ what it costs and how to make it pay for itself

£7.99 Paperback 0 7494 2234 3
160 pages March 1997

How to Cut Your Tax Bill
Without Breaking The Law
Third Edition
Grant Thornton

This jargon free guide unravels the complexities of the Inland Revenue and reveals ways for everyone to minimise their tax bill legally.

Bang up-to-date with new tax legislation **How to Cut Your Tax Bill** is the most succinct source of tax-saving tips available.

"a practical guide to all aspects of tax"

SUNDAY TIMES

"packed with information on how the tax system works"

GLOUCESTERSHIRE ECHO

£7.99 Paperback 0 7494 2016 2
176 pages March 1997

Available from all good book shops or to obtain further information please contact the publishers at the address below:

Kogan Page Ltd
Pentonville Road, London N1 9JN
Tel: 0171 278 0433, Fax: 0171 837 6348

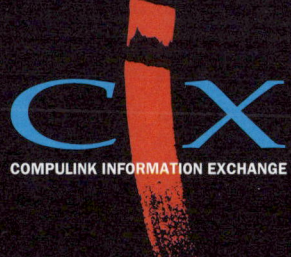

THE ORIGINAL & ULTIMATE HOME OFFICE

With today's technology more and more people are opting to work from home, saving precious, hard-earned money and releasing them from the tensions and stresses of daily commuting.

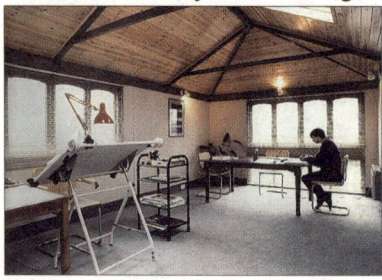

But often there is a space problem, the 'den' being too small for serious business and the spare bedroom not such a good option when guests suddenly descend upon you.

Today's houses are rarely designed to take extensions and those that take the plunge to build one, often find the result unsatisfactory and uneconomical. The building work creates dust, dirt and inconvenience for a prolonged period, often longer than anticipated, with the additional costs escalating.

The solution is brilliantly simple. Peter Bolger, Managing Director of Homelodge Buildings, has conceived and developed a highly versatile, practical and cost-effective alternative, The Homelodge.

Homelodge is timber-framed, fully insulated as well as double-glazed and is designed to be free standing on concrete padstones. The Bolger family run business started production over 10 years ago and now offers a choice of Homelodge designs starting from the 12' x 12' Cinnabar at a cost of £7,100. Prices include delivery of the sections, on-site assembly in a matter of days, lighting, heating, internal and external decoration.

Each Homelodge is aesthetically designed to enhance rather than detract from its surroundings, usually the garden. With the number of people working from home steadily rising, the demands for extra space to integrate an office, studio, workroom or leisure space, increases. The flexibility of this concept is demonstrated by the variety of uses already adopted throughout the country, offices, granny annexes, playrooms, artist, craft and musicians studios, surgeries and even a book repository for a publisher.

The uses are limitless and, on the whole, planning permission is not necessary. There are always exceptions, particularly if you happen to live in a conservation area, an area of outstanding natural beauty or a listed building. However, part of the Homelodge service is to deal with any possible planning implications.

Homelodge is designed by architects and built to housing standards.

Using best quality materials Homelodge components are prefabricated in the factory. All external timbers are treated with preservative to provide lasting protection. Homelodge is a warm and cosy building having double glazing and 4" of mineral wool insulation in the suspended floor, walls and roof. These factors combine to make Homelodge unique in that it is so well insulated that it can be comfortably used throughout the year.

Gone are the days of worrying about extra costs that may be sprung upon you. You will know the cost at the time of order, there are no hidden extras on Homelodge and little on-going maintenance.

If you are using your Homelodge for business purposes, you may be able to reclaim the VAT element. Homelodge is wonderful value for money (finance is available by additional mortgage or bank loan for this sound investment).

For full details telephone HOMELODGE BUILDINGS LTD (01962) 881480.

THE☆EXPRESS Guides:

Your Money
How to Make the Most of it (Second Edition)
Niki Chesworth

◆ a practical, reliable guide aimed at cutting through financial jargon
◆ invaluable advice on everything from banking and taxes to retirement
◆ essential to make your money work for you

£7.99 Paperback 0 7494 1641 6
128 pages 1995

Be Your Own Boss!
How to Set Up a Successful Small Business
David McMullan

◆ lays out all the facts you need to know before choosing and setting up your own business
◆ highlights common problems and potential minefields in a new business

£7.99 Paperback 0 7494 1187 2
128 pages 1994

Great Ideas for Making Money
Niki Chesworth

◆ 70 inspiring ideas on making money from antiques dealing to window cleaning
◆ advice on how to turn your ideas into profits

£7.99 Paperback 0 7494 1188 0
224 pages 1994

You And The Law
A Simple Guide to all Your Legal Problems
Susan Singleton

◆ a jargon free guide to remove the confusion surrounding the legal system
◆ practical advice on everything from tax and employment rights to divorce
◆ advice on how to deal with solicitors and legal actions

£6.99 Paperback 0 7494 1133 0
120 pages 1994

Available from all good book shops or to obtain further information please contact the publishers at the address below:

Kogan Page Ltd
Pentonville Road, London N1 9JN
Tel: 0171 278 0433, Fax: 0171 837 6348

There are a number of preventative measures that you can take to ensure peace of mind, for instance, taking out a maintenance contract. Some people regard these as being similar to insurance – you either take a risk that the equipment won't go wrong or you choose the careful route. It doesn't quite work like that though. In practice, if your equipment goes wrong and you do not have a maintenance contract, you are likely to be put on the bottom of the urgency pile of any repair company you phone up – they usually give priority to those customers with contracts. This may not be a problem if the technology is not vital to your everyday business, but if it is, you will end up with a major problem. Call-out times of two to three weeks are not uncommon! This can be more costly than even the labour and replacement spare parts costs.

For this reason, it is worth taking out a maintenance contract for your vital components, typically the computer, fax, printer and modem.

Most equipment comes with a minimum 12 months' warranty and many manufacturers are now including three years' warranty either as standard or available for an additional fee (this reflects the growing reliability of technology).

In addition to the standard warranty, you should also seriously consider an on-site maintenance contract. In other words, the repair company will come to your home office to fix the equipment. This has two main advantages; first, it saves you the cost of packing up and sending back the equipment and second, you are likely to have it up and running again more quickly. You can often take out such a service when you buy your piece of equipment; usually for the first year the price is quite modest, while in the subsequent years, prices typically come out at around 5 per cent of the original purchase price of the equipment. Companies usually quote a maximum call-out time of four to eight hours to get to you.

A little care has to be taken when signing up for such contracts: you should read the small print quite carefully. Check what the call-out times are and that the cost is fully inclusive of replacement of all parts and labour. Check also that the repair will actually be carried out in your home. In many cases this is usually possible; however, it has been known for some companies to offer an 'on-site' service, but all they do is pick the equipment up and take it away for repair.

Your health and your computer

There is concern in some quarters that computer screens can have a bad effect on health, and European legislation has been formulated to attack this. When buying your computer screen, it is worth taking this point seriously and enquiring whether the screen will conform to this legislation. Some further tips:

First, if you already have a computer, you can buy an anti-glare cover that attaches to the front of the screen, helping to cut down harmful emissions and remove static electricity and glare from room lighting. They cost around £40.

Second, some people are sensitive to particular colours on the computer screen, which can give rise to headaches. This can be remedied by changing the screen colours within the software packages that you are using.

Third, position your room lighting (both artificial and natural) so you minimise the glare, otherwise it puts additional strain on the eyes. In the case of nearby windows, it may well be useful to install blinds so that you can reduce glare and contrast in bright sunlight.

Lastly, seating; screen and keyboard positions must be chosen carefully to avoid poor posture and body strain. Many people are concerned about the risks associated with repetitive strain injuries (RSI) which arise for a number of reasons, including lengthy repetitive motion and awkward body positions and pressure on nerves and muscles. Some basic rules of thumb for avoiding problems are:

- Maintain the screen at or slightly below eye level.
- Keep the keyboard flat and close to your elbow level.
- Ensure the work surface is at a height to allow your elbows to be relaxed and your knees to fit underneath.
- Your feet should either be placed flat on the floor or on a foot rest.
- Your chair should be sloped slightly forward so that your knees are slightly lower than your hips.
- Make sure your back is upright or slightly inclined forward from the hips.
- Your head should be directly over your shoulders and about an arm's length from the screen.
- Ensure that your neck and shoulders are relaxed.
- Every 20–40 minutes, take a short break and perform some hands, shoulders and neck stretching exercises.

Further information about current health and safety guidelines is available from the government Health and Safety Executive (see page 211).

Keep your equipment cool and ventilated

Most technology can cope with wide changes in temperature. In the UK we do not have the extremes of temperature common in some countries. But direct sunlight on equipment can have a disastrous effect. It can build up extremely high temperatures and do permanent damage. So avoid any direct sunlight on equipment and, to state the obvious, the sun does move, and what is a cool location for equipment in the morning can turn out to be a hot-bed in the afternoon!

Many pieces of technology have ventilation holes and fans fitted to help keep the equipment inside the casing cool. Again, it may be stating the obvious, but the ventilation holes must be kept free, otherwise the equipment casing will turn into an oven. Read the manufacturer's instructions and leave the right air gaps around this area.

Power

We all take for granted that the mains supply will always be there, but occasionally our illusions are shattered with power cuts. As these events are rare, it is probably best to take a philosophical approach when they happen, and wait for the power supply to return.

Alternatively, you could buy an uninterruptable power supply, which, in simple terms, is a big battery which will immediately take over from the mains supply if it fails. How much they cost depends upon how much power you need and how long you want the battery to last. Typically, prices start at £100 for which you will gain anything upwards of 10 minutes of battery life, and rise considerably with battery lifetime.

Probably of more use is a power protection device, which protects your equipment from power surges and 'spikes' in the mains supply. This really is worth the expense, as occasional mains problems can do serious damage to a computer, including destroying all your hard disc's data. These devices look rather like a five-way mains adaptor board, allowing you to plug in five different pieces of equipment, and they cost between £30 and £110, depending on how many pieces of equipment you want to protect.

Protection from computer viruses

Computer viruses are rather like the electronic equivalent of the medical kind: software programs that the less socially minded members of the computer world have invented to bring misery to computer users. The software programs are not easily detectable by normal computer usage and are designed to act rather like a ship's stowaway – transferring from one computer to another without the users realising, typically when normal software is copied on to floppy discs and transferred to another computer. Viruses can have disastrous effects on computers, including completely destroying all data on the hard disc. One common way of acquiring them is through games software. There is no guaranteed way of avoiding them and even software suppliers have fallen foul and accidentally supplied 'infected' programs, though some ways to minimise the risk are:

- Always use software that you have bought from a recognised dealer.
- Be particularly aware that software that is downloaded from on-line computers (eg the Internet) may be infected with viruses.
- Beware of illegal copying of software (more about this later).
- Buy virus detection software that will help you do a 'medical check' on your computer on a regular basis and which will also perform a 'cure' (this type of software needs to be regularly up-dated to ensure it keeps up with the latest viruses). Virus detection software can also be set up to continuously monitor the files on your computer, alerting you to a problem the minute it detects a new virus.

Locking the computer up

You may want to have a facility to lock your PC so that only you can gain access to it, which can be particularly important with a portable PC. Many computers come with a key-lock already installed, so look out for this when choosing. An alternative is to use software that has password protection, so that only you can gain access.

Copying software

In the same way as it is illegal to copy music from records and compact discs, it is also illegal to copy other people's software and use it. The only exception to this rule is the use of shareware software, where the developers of this low-cost software encourage users to copy it to other people, with the condition that if it is then used, they should contact the developers and pay a low-cost fee.

Not only is copying illegal, but it is also not in your best interests. If you buy such software, first you are open to prosecution and second, you will not have access to the software manuals and any hot-line telephone support for the product. This is a serious disadvantage, so avoid the 'cheap-skate' route!

A grey area does exist (as with many aspects of new technologies) and that relates to using software if you have both a desktop machine and a portable. In theory, when you 'buy' software, you are usually only purchasing a right to use it yourself (a subtle difference), though some software suppliers are demanding that you need to buy a copy both for the desktop and portable machine, even though there are not many instances when you have two pairs of hands to operate them at the same time. The more enlightened companies are beginning to realise this now and accept that you can install the software on both machines, provided you only ever use one at a time .

Regular data back-ups

It's a fact of life that we all set out with the good intention of making regular back-up copies of our computer data, but somehow, day-to-day business matters get in the way. You can go for more than a year without a problem (lulling you into a false sense of security) and suddenly you turn on your machine and you can't find anything. It's not a pleasant feeling as what has happened sinks in.

Back-ups of your data can be very simply performed by copying it on to floppy discs on a regular basis. It is often a good idea to do a daily, weekly and monthly back-up, each on separate sets of discs. That way, if you lose both your daily and weekly copies, at least you have the monthly ones. It is also a good idea to make back-up copies of your software program files and even keep these in a separate location, for example at a friend's house. In that way, if you have a burglary or fire, you will be able to get back into action pretty quickly with a new PC.

If you want to make the job a lot easier, you could buy what is called a tape back-up system. This is a magnetic tape device that will copy all the data from your hard disc on to tapes, copying absolutely everything on the hard disc, and saving the need to use many different floppy discs. Such devices make the process of saving data simple, fast and easy, which will encourage you to do backups on a regular basis. Prices start at around £100.

There are also software tools to help you back up your data, making it simpler, quicker and more organised. This software is usually referred to as utility software and typically includes other features to help you organise your data.

Keep it clean

It's surprising how dirty equipment can get in everyday use; from time to time it is worth doing a 'spring-clean', to keep surfaces and ventilation holes free from dust and dirt. But do remember to follow the manufacturer's instructions on cleaning materials.

Data Protection Act

You may want to keep details of people on your computer's database, eg, for mailing purposes. The Data Protection Act requires you to register, with the intention of protecting the public from the misuse of computerised personal information (and quite right too!). A publication exists called 'The Data Protection Act: The Simpler Way for Small Businesses to Register' (telephone number for enquiries is given on page 211).

11

Bits and pieces

The recurring theme of much of this book is that technology tools can help you to improve the efficiency of how you work – after all there are only a finite number of working hours in the day. While many of the major tools described require some initial effort in choosing and getting to know them, there are also a number of cheapish and useful tools that will complement them – and make your life that little bit easier. This chapter outlines some of the tools available which may loosely be described under the technology banner.

Binding machines

If you need to produce high-quality reports or bound brochures, it can be very useful to have a binding machine in your home office. These machines will punch a series of holes in your pages and allow you to bind a document to produce a professional finish. You can include a report cover on the front and back, using stiff (and possibly laminated) card bought from most stationers. Furthermore, if you want to be really classy, you can go to your local printers to produce your own person-alised report covers – with your business name and logo included (Chapter 9 describes how to produce the artwork for this). The actual binding strips come in a variety of sizes, suitable for different quantities of pages.

For a good quality binding machine, prices start at around £120. Owning such a machine has several advantages over visits to the local stationers to have documents bound. First, it can work out more economical if you use it frequently and second, it is a lot quicker. In practice, speed can be a problem; it is an unwritten rule that just when you need a document bound in order to catch the last post, the stationers will be closing for the day!

Lamination machines

Sometimes you may come across the need to produce promotional literature, business cards, badges etc, where a high-quality look is desirable. Lamination machines will add a thin, clear plastic coating to your document and provide added protection from dirt, grease and grime. Machines typically cost £300 to buy, with each laminated sheet costing between 10 and 40 pence.

Scales and the post

Most stationers will sell you a set of scales for weighing letters and packets. At the end of the working day, it can save you waiting in a long queue in your local post office. You will also need a list of postal charges (both national and international) – the post office will provide this. But make sure you always have the most up-to-date prices and a large collection of different value stamps. Scales will set you back about £25.

Dictation machine

When you are out and about, you may find it useful to keep a portable dictation machine for taking notes, for instance when you are on a train journey. They are useful for noting ideas and thoughts that come up when you least expect them. One home-based worker who has ideas and inspiration at the oddest times (often when he is drinking in the local pub) found a different solution – he phones his own answerphone and records his thoughts which he feels he might forget after several pints of Young's special bitter.

Colour Letraset

If you want to add a touch of colour to your documents and can't afford a colour printer, it's worth considering buying a colour Letraset system. It allows you to 'iron on' colour letters to a page, using a small machine. Provided you are talking about small numbers, this can be a relatively cheap way of adding that 'final touch' to a document. Machines cost around £80.

Bulk letter mailing

Your business may require you to send out large quantities of letters on a regular basis. You can buy a small machine to help you with this; it will automatically fold letters, invoices and statements to fit your envelopes, though it is only worth it if you really do have large quantities! They cost around £150 – £200.

If you have this need, it is also worth talking to your local post office about their services for helping you to post large quantities of letters, including franking machines to save you having to stick stamps on to each letter.

Sticky labels

In addition to your standard PC printer, you may find that a small separate label printing machine could be useful. It connects to your PC and is used to generate address labels for sticking on envelopes. These machines come with software that allows you to automatically print a label while you are still using your word-processing software. They cost around £200.

Photocopier

In the early days of photocopiers, you had to be very careful about signing contracts as it was not always a simple case of buying one outright. You often had to pay rental on a per copy basis with contracts that were very difficult to extricate yourself from. However, it is now possible to buy them outright for as little as £500. You can of course spend a lot more, getting facilities for different paper sizes, quality of copy, copying speed and even including colour, though these more expensive machines are rarely worth buying for the home-based business. There are, after all, many printing and photocopying services around the country which are in most cases more cost effective.

12

Practical tips for home working

The ways in which people start to work from home are as many and varied as the businesses themselves. Some have a very clear idea of where they are going – they want more freedom to work for themselves; an alternative to the corporate world; more flexible working hours in order to fit in with children's schooling; taking advantage of flexible working possibilities with corporations. Or it may not be intentional – sudden redundancies may give little alternative. In any of these cases, the impact can be tremendous, not only on your work, but also on your whole lifestyle. The personal and social implications of working from home are only just beginning to be appreciated.

Adapting to this changing lifestyle will vary considerably from one person to another. The secret is to be aware of the differences and, from time to time, to re-evaluate how things are going, to identify what is good and bad about it and what changes you need to make. All of this can be very new to most people, particularly if you have been used to working in a large corporation where routines and ways of working are forced upon you. *You have to decide what is best for yourself*, and to think originally about how best to arrange your lifestyle.

Most books and articles on this subject only scratch the surface. The academics and psychologists tend to be rather negative about it all – simply raising all the bad points, without providing any helpful, original and positive advice. They also tend to approach it from a black and white perspective – you either work from home full time or you don't. In practice this is rarely the case; for instance, many businesses necessitate your spending much of your time with customers and suppliers. There are many positive aspects to working from home: you can arrange meetings outside rush hours, keeping the stress level low; you won't suffer from constant interruptions from colleagues; you have more flexibility to arrange your business and home life to suit yourself; you have more control over the business; you won't be clogging up over-crowded roads and polluting the atmosphere with daily car journeys. The list could go on.

But home working will not suit everyone. It does require certain characteristics, such as flexibility, an ability to adapt, an open mind and self-motivation and reliance. This chapter gives a few useful pointers on how these characteristics can be used to ensure you get the most out of home working.

Making your own rules and routines

Working in a traditional job imposes a whole range of rules, regulations and routines, and though the trend is for management styles that give ever-increasing responsibility to the individual, there are nevertheless many areas of work where rules and regulations predominate. Once you start working from home, this changes overnight. Suddenly you have, on the surface, complete freedom to do as you want. Unfortunately, this illusion is quickly shattered once you realise the full implications of having no regular pay cheque. Furthermore, if you have been used to having a vast array of support services around you in a large company, it is likely that having to do all these yourself will also be a shock to the system.

Most established home workers discover the need to develop a set of rules and routines, to help maximise their working time and to make sure they have 'play-time'. It is all to easy to forget the need for play, and it is particularly important for the home worker, where home and office are so close together. But never forget that one of the best things about making the rules yourself is that you can occasionally break them when an unexpected invitation to play happens!

One of the other benefits of making the rules is that you can design them to suit yourself. You may be a 'morning' person – working well between 8am and 1pm, but not at your best just after lunch. If this is the case, you can organise your workload to take account of this, for instance, doing the creative jobs in the morning and the more mundane administration ones, that don't require much thinking, after lunch. Other people are night owls and prefer to start work mid-morning and carry on late into the evening – each one to his or her own.

These rules and routines are particularly important when things are not going well – you may be having a problem with a customer, or there's not enough money coming in; the routines help you keep your head down through such periods.

Keeping your head down

It is highly likely that when you first start home working you will invent all sorts of excuses to avoid getting down to work, from cleaning the home to buying the shopping. The point is that it is very easy to get distracted, particularly if you are tackling a difficult subject or if things are not going well. A few tips then:

- Once you have got up in the morning go to your office as soon as it is practical and start work.
- Don't leave the office until your next break, ie lunchtime (even for making coffee or tea – make a thermos flask for the whole morning instead).
- If you do have to make a break from work, leave whatever you are doing not fully complete – that way you have something to come straight back into when you return (it's easier to get back into the swing of things this way).
- Each day, make a list of the things you want to get done and tick them off as you go, but be realistic. If you start out with too high an expectation of what you will achieve, you will always be disappointed.
- Set priorities of what you need to get done.
- Some days you will find good, others bad. Try to determine what are the factors that dictate this for you (for example lack of sleep is not much good for the creative process) and try to work these practicalities into appropriate tasks for the day.
- Allocate some time each week to evaluating how you are doing (what's going well, what isn't) and for thinking of new ideas for the business. Talk to others about your ideas and get opinions, particularly from people not in your direct line of work; sometimes they can bring surprisingly objective and constructive ideas as they can 'stand back' from your everyday involvement in the business.
- If you are having difficulties with a particular job, try an easier task first – the difficult one may then fall into place.
- If you are working late into the night and are struggling with a particular issue, leave it and sleep on it; you'll be amazed at the effect a night's sleep can have in clarifying a problem.
- When you are fed up and things are not going well, this is more than ever the time to keep your head down and keep to your set of rules and routines – be tough on yourself.

Social contacts

One of the most important issues about home working is that it can lead to isolation. We all perhaps take for granted the social contact when working with other people in traditional businesses. The joys of not being bothered by interruptions from colleagues can quickly lead to a sense of loss – from the gossip and discussions about social events to the exchange of ideas about jobs and business. This must not be underestimated and it is important to find a replacement to suit your degree of self-sufficiency.

My own business involves many meetings with clients each week and this provides much social contact. In fact, it is always pleasing to get back to the home office to have peace and quiet for working on reports. But there are times when there are several days on the trot without client meetings, and these periods of calm have led to the formation of The Balham Luncheon Society – a collection of home-based workers in South London. We get together on an ad-hoc basis for lunch or early evening drinks. This may sound trivial, but it is important to one's sanity in home working. But there are other benefits – our growing band of home workers have suddenly found that we can work together and give each other business. It's the start of a new wave of home business networking.

This is one idea that suits a particular group of people. Whatever your solution to social contact, don't underestimate the need for it and, if you can, work it in to your business life. Make contact with other home workers, for instance by putting adverts in the local paper. Alternatively, take advantage of flexible working hours and go to the local sports club during the day when it does not have the weekend rush. Think originally and openly – after all, you don't have the constraints of a normal job.

Other issues

Numerous other issues on the subject of home working exist, a major one being how to deal with the family and, in particular, children. Many people believe that one of the advantages of working from home is that it answers the problem of combining a career and home life with the kids. This is, however, anything but the case. Sure, the flexible hours can allow you to take the kids to school and pick them up, but as for spending time with them during the day – this is generally a no-no.

Children of all ages will demand attention and it is impractical to think that you can make your business work and give attention to children at the same time.

Partners can be just as much a problem and how to deal with them depends on many factors, such as who the principal bread winner is, whether you are both at home, how your relationship works generally, the degree of equality in the relationship and so on. The important thing is to anticipate both the problems and the opportunities and adapt and develop the relationship to create a lifestyle that suits both partners.

13

Useful vocabulary

Compact disc (CD): Trademark name for compact disc technology originally developed by Philips and Sony.

Compact disc audio (CD-audio): The domestic market product for distribution of audio information.

Compact disc interactive (CD-I): A consumer electronics product – the multimedia compact disc player that plugs into a TV and hi-fi and which plays CD-I discs that contain text, graphics, animations, pictures, music and video.

Compact disc read only memory (CD-ROM): The compact disc storage system for computer data (it cannot be written to directly from a computer).

Database: Software for organising and quickly retrieving information.

Desktop video telephony: A capability to use a desktop computer as a video-telephone.

Disc operating system (DOS): The industry standard format for control of storage media by PCs, eg floppy and hard discs.

Dot matrix printer: A low-cost printer for a PC.

Electronic mail (e-mail): Information/mail sent electronically.

Floppy disc: A low-capacity magnetic storage medium for computer data.

Front-end: The first part of computer software that a user will see.

Generic: In software terms, material that is broadly applicable to a wide audience.

Graphics: Non-textual information on a PC such as illustrations, icons and drawings.

Hard disc: A medium-capacity magnetic storage device for computer data.

Hardware: The physical components of computer systems.

Ink-jet printer: A medium quality printer for the PC.

Internet: The international 'network of networks' linking computers and computer networks around the world.

ISDN: Integrated Services Digital Network: The new broadband all-digital telecommunications network.

Laser printer: A high-quality printer for printing text, graphics and images, that uses laser technology.

Multimedia: The combination of text, numbers, graphics, pictures, audio and video on a single computer.

Optical disc: A high-capacity data storage medium, based on optical technology.

Personal Computer (PC): A trademark of IBM Corporation, though in this book, personal computer is taken in its broadest sense to include any brand.

Photo-CD: Kodak's service for conversion of 35mm transparencies and negatives into digital format on a CD-ROM.

Presentation graphics software: Software that allows you to prepare drawings and illustrations.

Scanner: A facility to scan paper documents, to convert them to a digital image, for processing electronically.

Software: The complement to hardware, which describes the programs and which controls a computer.

Spreadsheet: Software which allows the manipulation of numbers.

Video Graphics Adaptor (VGA): An interface card for displaying medium resolution graphics on a suitable screen.

Windows: A trademark of the Microsoft Corporation for its windows software environment.

Word-processing: Software principally for the manipulation of text.

14

Additional information

Computer magazines

The following magazines are available from newsagents:

- *Computer Buyer*
- *Computer Shopper*
- *Personal Computer World*
- *PC Answers*
- *PC Direct*
- *PC Magazine*
- *PC User*
- *What Micro?*
- *What Personal Computer?*
- *Which Computer?*

Other useful books, magazines and publications

- *Which?* – magazine, carries out technology reviews from time to time
- *Live Wire* (quarterly magazine for teleworkers) – Regent Publishing, 35 Brent Street, London NW4 2EF
- *The New Homeworkers*, Ursula Huws (Low Pay Unit, 1984)
- 'Impacts of Computer-Mediated Home-Based Work on Women and Their Families', Kathleen Christensen (*Office: Technology and People*, November 1987)
- 'Home Truths About Teleworking', John and Celia Stanworth (*Personnel Management*, November 1989)
- 'Promoting Work/Family Balance', Douglas Hall (*Organisational Dynamics*, 1990)
- 'Planning Permission for Small Businesses – A Step by Step Guide' (Department of the Environment)

Electronic information providers

- CompuServe (tel: 0800 289378)
- FT Profile (tel: 01932 787231)
- ICC Information Services (tel: 0181 783 1122)
- Infocheck (tel: 0171 377 8872)
- Jordan & Sons (tel: 0171 253 3030)
- Kompass On-line (tel: 01342 326972)
- Reuters Textline (tel: 0171 250 1122)

Telecommunications companies

The two major telecommunications companies are:

- British Telecom (dial 100 and ask for Freephone Telecom Sales)
- Mercury (freephone 0800 424 194)

or, if available, your local cable TV company.

Organisations

- Health & Safety Executive – Information relating to health and safety at work (tel: 0171 221 0870)
- Office of the Data Protection Registrar (tel: 01625 535777)
- ACRE (Association of Rural Community Councils in England) – contact Alan Denbigh (tel: 0145 383 4874). They have set up a project to develop interest in teleworking in country areas of England
- Telecommuting Powerhouse (tel: 0171 404 5011)
- Federation of Small Businesses (tel: 0171 928 9272)
- Alliance of Small Firms (tel: 01249 817003)
- Confereration of British Industry (CBI) – Small Firms Council (tel: 0171 379 7400)
- Department of Trade and Industry – Small Firms Division (tel: 01742 597508)
- National Association of Teleworkers (tel: 01761 413869)
- British Insurance & Investment Brokers Association (0171 623 9043)
- Legal Protection Group (0171 661 1491)

Index

Index of Advertisers

THE EXPRESS

Your Home Office
Third Edition
Peter Chatterton

If you plan to run a business from home or use a room there for occasional freelance work, you will need a copy of **Your Home Office.**

It describes how to choose and set up an office that will enable you to work efficiently, productively and profitably. Topics covered include:

◆ what basic equipment can provide the facilities of a modern office

◆ what it costs and how to make it pay for itself

£7.99 Paperback 0 7494 2234 3
160 pages March 1997

How to Cut Your Tax Bill
Without Breaking The Law
Third Edition
Grant Thornton

This jargon free guide unravels the complexities of the Inland Revenue and reveals ways for everyone to minimise their tax bill legally.

Bang up-to-date with new tax legislation **How to Cut Your Tax Bill** is the most succinct source of tax-saving tips available.

"a practical guide to all aspects of tax"

SUNDAY TIMES

"packed with information on how the tax system works"

GLOUCESTERSHIRE ECHO

£7.99 Paperback 0 7494 2016 2
176 pages March 1997

Available from all good book shops or to obtain further information please contact the publishers at the address below:

Kogan Page Ltd
Pentonville Road, London N1 9JN
Tel: 0171 278 0433, Fax: 0171 837 6348

THE EXPRESS

Titles from The Express series

NEW

The Express Investment Guide
Practical Advice for Making the Right Choice
Second Edition
Tony Levene

Do you find the choice of investment options now on offer bewildering? Do you want some impartial, clear advice on the pros and cons of the various alternatives available? If so then **The Express Investment Guide** is for you.

Well informed and jargon free, this guide covers the full range of investment choices for individuals, looking at everything from building societies and banks to the stock market. Essential for anyone wanting to save or invest a sum, however large or small.

£7.99 Paperback ISBN 0 7494 2015 4
128 pages March 1997

The Express Guide to Buying a Property Abroad
A Practical Guide for Overseas Homebuyers
Second Edition
Niki Chesworth

Do you dream of living abroad? Whether as a second home or a permanent residence, more and more people are turning such a dream into reality. Written in a clear, down-to-earth style **The Express Guide to Buying a Property Abroad** pinpoints the common pitfalls that can make the dream a nightmare. Every area is covered, including:

◆ a detailed country-by-country guide
◆ a thorough assessment of all the costs and benefits of moving
◆ a discussion of the different ways of buying

£7.99 Paperback ISBN 0 7494 2017 0
184 pages March 1997

Available from all good book shops or to obtain further information please contact the publishers at the address below:

Kogan Page Ltd
Pentonville Road, London N1 9JN
Tel: 0171 278 0433, Fax: 0171 837 6348

THE EXPRESS Guides:

Your Money
How to Make the Most of it (Second Edition)
Niki Chesworth

♦ a practical, reliable guide aimed at cutting through financial jargon
♦ invaluable advice on everything from banking and taxes to retirement
♦ essential to make your money work for you

£7.99 Paperback 0 7494 1641 6
128 pages 1995

Be Your Own Boss!
How to Set Up a Successful Small Business
David McMullan

♦ lays out all the facts you need to know before choosing and setting up your own business
♦ highlights common problems and potential minefields in a new business

£7.99 Paperback 0 7494 1187 2
128 pages 1994

Great Ideas for Making Money
Niki Chesworth

♦ 70 inspiring ideas on making money from antiques dealing to window cleaning
♦ advice on how to turn your ideas into profits

£7.99 Paperback 0 7494 1188 0
224 pages 1994

You And The Law
A Simple Guide to all Your Legal Problems
Susan Singleton

♦ a jargon free guide to remove the confusion surrounding the legal system
♦ practical advice on everything from tax and employment rights to divorce
♦ advice on how to deal with solicitors and legal actions

£6.99 Paperback 0 7494 1133 0
120 pages 1994

Available from all good book shops or to obtain further information please contact the publishers at the address below:

Kogan Page Ltd
Pentonville Road, London N1 9JN
Tel: 0171 278 0433, Fax: 0171 837 6348

THE ⊕ EXPRESS

Your Home Office
Third Edition
Peter Chatterton

If you plan to run a business from home or use a room there for occasional freelance work, you will need a copy of **Your Home Office**.

It describes how to choose and set up an office that will enable you to work efficiently, productively and profitably. Topics covered include:

◆ what basic equipment can provide the facilities of a modern office

◆ what it costs and how to make it pay for itself

£7.99 Paperback 0 7494 2234 3
160 pages March 1997

How to Cut Your Tax Bill
Without Breaking The Law
Third Edition
Grant Thornton

This jargon free guide unravels the complexities of the Inland Revenue and reveals ways for everyone to minimise their tax bill legally.

Bang up-to-date with new tax legislation **How to Cut Your Tax Bill** is the most succinct source of tax-saving tips available.

"a practical guide to all aspects of tax"

SUNDAY TIMES

"packed with information on how the tax system works"

GLOUCESTERSHIRE ECHO

£7.99 Paperback 0 7494 2016 2
176 pages March 1997

Available from all good book shops or to obtain further information please contact the publishers at the address below:

Kogan Page Ltd
Pentonville Road, London N1 9JN
Tel: 0171 278 0433, Fax: 0171 837 6348